AROUND
the
WATER
TANK

Memories of a Mid-Century Mill Village

JAMES C. HAIGLER

Note for Librarians: A cataloguing record for this book is available from Library and Archives
Canada at www.collectionscanada.ca/amicus/index-e.html
ISBN 1-4120-9294-9

Printed in Victoria, BC, Canada. Printed on paper with minimum 30% recycled fibre.
Trafford's print shop runs on "green energy" from solar, wind and other environmentally-friendly power sources.

TRAFFORD
PUBLISHIN

Offices in Canada, USA, Ireland and UK

Book sales for North America and international:
Trafford Publishing, 6E–2333 Government St.,
Victoria, BC V8T 4P4 CANADA
phone 250 383 6864 (toll-free 1 888 232 4444)
fax 250 383 6804; email to orders@trafford.com
Book sales in Europe:
Trafford Publishing (UK) Limited, 9 Park End Street, 2nd Floor
Oxford, UK OX1 1HH UNITED KINGDOM
phone 44 (0)1865 722 113 (local rate 0845 230 9601)
facsimile 44 (0)1865 722 868; info.uk@trafford.com
Order online at:
trafford.com/06-1048

10 9 8 7 6 5 4

Dedication

<u>To My Beautiful Wife</u>

Jane
*Whose continued encouragement and
support made it possible
for this collection to come to fruition*

<u>Our Children</u>

Michael and Alan Haigler
&
Kathryn and John Bumgarner
*Their unique character traits brought life
and personality to the Stories*

<u>To the Memory of</u>

Hayne and Frances Haigler
&
Evelyn Watkins "Sister"
*Who raised my brother David and me
in the Atco Mill Village*

Acknowledgements

<u>Main Characters</u>

Boyce Thomas
*A pediatrician in Newnan, Georgia who was my
next-door neighbor for eight years in the Atco Mill Village*

Cliff Dyar
*My old snake-catching buddy who is retired from the
FBI after twenty-five years of service and now lives in Arkansas*

<u>Special Thanks</u>

The Bartow Trader
Rick Richardson, Editor
*For providing a live readership by printing
excerpts of* Around the Water Tank

Louise Weldon and Jamie Harrison
*For their assistance in editing and proofing which
made the publication of this collection possible*

Bartow History Center
*The aerial photograph on the back cover was
provided from the collection of the Bartow History Center*

Tonsmeire Studio
*Louis Tonsmeire of Tonsmeire Studios is responsible for
the cover and author's photographs*

Kim DeReuter
*For her expertise and patience in creating
the wonderful cover design and graphics*

Introduction

The seeds for this venture were sewn in the waning minutes of a sweaty July afternoon as I sat on our front porch swing with my wife Jane. The recent rain shower left a steamy haze hovering over the still warm asphalt paving. Between the hanging ferns I caught a glimpse of a tiny tow-headed girl playing with a large Styrofoam glider that was almost as big a she was.

As I watched her frolic, my mind began filling with memories of constructing the model planes we flew back when I was a kid in the late forties and early fifties. I got a pad and pen and began to scribble down some notes as these images from the past flooded my mind.

Over time, events of the present day would occasionally trail back to other childhood scenes, and more stories began to coalesce. Most take place in or around the Atco Mill Village where I lived from 1945 until we moved in 1957 during my eighth grade year. The yarns include the games we enjoyed, the trips we took, the people we knew, and the challenges we faced during the post World War II era.

We played outside in all kinds of weather with the simplest of props. A discarded tin can fished from the garbage was the centerpiece of one of our favorite games, "Kick the Can", that provided hours of entertainment. A discarded broom handle was a treasure. It could become a sword, a gun, a horse, a bat, or a multitude of other implements needed for whatever diversion our youthful imaginations could conceive. Even the spring seeds of the silver maple, that we called whirlybirds, could keep us occupied all afternoon.

The focal point of our young lives in the village was the playground at the side of the grammar school. The swing sets, seesaws, merry-go-round, and slide provided year-round amusement. On the other side of the school was the most cherished venue for summer play – the pool. It had white ceramic tile with a ten-foot high diving board at the deep end and a slide that spanned over the baby pool at the other. It was drained and cleaned each week and refilled with well water. The swimming pool was crystal clear, but icy cold.

We rode our bikes, skated, flew kites, played baseball, fished, hunted bottles, and caught snakes at the creeks that flanked the village. Doors were never locked, and we felt at home in the houses of our friends. We were just as likely to get a spanking from a neighbor for misbehaving as from our own parents.

We had no air conditioning, cell phones, computers, video games, or automatic automobile transmissions. My family got our first television when I was nine with only one station on the air, and it broadcast in glorious black and white.

The water tank, or tower as it is more accurately called, was the focal point of the immaculately maintained park in front of the Goodyear Mill in Atco. It was the landmark that welcomed us home after a long journey and a target for occasional graffiti.

Towns all over the country had water towers that proudly announced their existence as you approached them en route to far away places. Being the first to spot the next tower along the way was a game we played to help pass the time while traveling.

The goal in writing this book has been to paint pictures of various aspects of village life during this time period through a series of humorous stories. Each is based on actual events and is as accurate as memory allows. A few have been enhanced a bit to include some things that almost happened and other things that we talked about doing but were chicken.

The Stories

One: **Model Student**

As I took my seat on the porch swing one late July evening, a lazy fog knelt over the warm asphalt street giving thanks to the much-needed rain that sprinkled the area moments earlier. I peered across the hazy street and witnessed a scene that sent me back many years to my childhood days growing up in the Atco Mill Village.

Through the mist, framed by carefully watered hanging-fern baskets and semi-conscious azaleas, I saw a diminutive, three-year-old girl with long, blond hair trailing down her back and following her every move. She was running circles around the neighbor's tiny, downtown, front yard, two houses down and across the road from my vantage point. Soon I realized that the object of her delight was a large, Styrofoam airplane, some three feet long with an equal wingspan.

She sprinted to and fro, releasing the airship at various angles, yielding results that varied from a sharp nose dive straight into the dirt to a gentle, dipping glide settling softly on the ground. She squealed almost continuously as she made her way across the yard, utterly disregarding the attitude in which the craft made its first contact with terra firma.

As I viewed this innocent romp, my mind drifted back in time as my tired body settled into the tilt and sway of the swing. Our model planes in the fifties came in small boxes barely an inch thick and about as wide as your hand. Some were as long as two feet, but most were well shy of that. They only weighed in at about three ounces. Each box sported a beautiful black and white picture tempting our imagination of how this soon-to-be flying machine would look sailing high above the trees.

It was discovered very quickly that the plastic propeller and pair of wheels heavily influenced the weight of the box. The thin, bent wire that would attach the wheels and the foot-long rubber band made up most of the remainder of the weight.

Other contents included several paper-thin sheets of what we soon learned was balsa wood. Some of the sheets contained patterns imprinted in blue ink while others sported thin strips attached at one end. A few thin pieces of folded tissue paper you could almost see through and the four-page, foldout directions completed the contents. All of these things would invariably blow off the "designated" card table every time the oscillating fan made a pass.

This old, well-worn table was only placed into service for a rare, three-table bridge party emergency hosted by my mother or Sister, my aunt who lived with us. For those occasions it would be fitted with a red, silky slipcover to disguise the glue residue and tattered wafer board top that I was allowed to use for my various aeronautical construction activities.

There were miles of balsa strips smaller than a toothpick that would become the skeletal struts of the fuselage, wings, and tail of the model. The thin pallets of struts came together at one end as if to say, "We belong together and are not intended for casual separation." Their unspoken wishes soon became apparent when I tried to free one of them from the solid end to begin the fuselage assembly.

A series of successively smaller circular shapes, with tiny notches were printed on one of the paper-thin balsa sheets. These cutouts would form the shape of the body once they were connected and spaced about two inches apart by the balsa struts. There was a hole in the center of each oval that was supposed to be cut out so the rubber band/engine could form its double knots and power the craft to unknown heights.

Had I been a brain surgeon, with all their tools at my disposal, I might have been able to trim those oblong, wafer thin fuselage pieces somewhere near the printed lines on the balsa. However, the little notches around the edges intended to receive the struts were beyond the realm of current technology.

At any rate using what tools I had available, including my dad's discarded double-edged razor blades, I made my boldest effort to follow the lines and clip out the small notches along the perimeter. On about the third balsa pancake carved, I realized why there were so many of those little strut strips in the box. They were to be used as braces across the grain of the delicate body ovals that broke as I tried to carve the twenty-five specified notches around their circumference AND cut out the half-inch hole in the center of each. (I didn't know I would run out of patience before actually installing the "engine".)

During the fuselage assembly phase, another important discovery was made. The Testors glue, that I paid extra for, dries a lot more quickly on your fingers, razor blades, tweezers, scissors, and other assembly aids than it does on the balsa wood and, therefore, sticks parts to everything except the other plane piece to which they were designed to stick.

At some point during the fourth week of construction, as I was cutting out the long, rounded pieces that formed the wing profile, I realized that if I was going to finish before summer was over I had to get creative.

As it turned out, a great new tool was right under my nose all the time, and because I was using the old, beat-up card table, I was allowed to put this new device into use.

My aunt, Sister, was into sewing and kept a handy cache of straight pins neatly stuck in place inside a folded, brown piece of paper with "Singer" written on it. These became my greatest ally. No longer did I have to hold two pieces together for half an hour for the glue to set; I just pinned it. Unfortunately, the glue adhered better to the pins than to the balsa.

By trial and error, I learned the trick of pinning the instructions to the table, then pinning the wing-shaped pieces to the instruction pattern, and finally cementing the struts to the wing pieces. Using this approach I was able to somewhat duplicate the intended wing profile. The only down side was that I had to delicately trim off all the instruction paper that stuck to the frame, because a square inch of it weighed more than the entire stack of tissue which was intended to form the skin. This extra weight on one side would make it difficult to achieve a plumb attitude during flight.

In the six weeks it had taken to complete the skeleton of this masterpiece, the beautiful, royal blue and white tissue paper that would form the plane's skin had been used to adorn somebody's August birthday present. Being of resourceful means, I climbed to the top shelf of the hall closet and wrestled down the Christmas wrapping box. There I was able to salvage several used pieces of tissue that would do the job nicely for my model. A little wrinkled from years of use (Who said recycling is a new thing?), but just enough to complete my labor of love.

To make matters worse, sometime during the summer, my little brother had managed to adapt the plastic wheels and wire axle of my model to make a tin-can automobile. Also, the rubber band had found its way around a large stack of some of Daddy's important papers.

Undaunted, I completed construction a few days before summer's end and decided to launch the new "glider" from the second-level reinforcing beam of the village water tower. Four steel latticed legs supported this large, silver cylinder a hundred and fifty feet in the air. It had a cone-shaped top and a rounded bottom with a narrow catwalk around the base of the tank. A blue band bisected the vessel with yellow lettering on each side that spelled out "GOODYEAR" which was split in the center by the famous winged-foot. It stood in the middle of the park in front of the mill and across the street from my house.

The park was filled with large hardwoods and several tall magnolias. Gravel paths lined with large rocks crisscrossed the pristine landscape, and lush shrubbery formed small sitting areas throughout the shaded, immaculately maintained grounds. These little hide-a-ways presented a great stage for haunting during the proper season, but that is another story.

As the sun went down on the last Sunday of August, the long shadows set the stage for my moment of glory. Word had spread around to the other kids in the village, and a crowd had gathered at the foot of the tower for the "launch." I made my way through the milling crowd and slowly ascended the steel rungs, looping my elbow around each, keeping a firm grasp on my trophy. I made it up to a point that was "high enough" but not quite to the second level.

Then, with all eyes upon my small frame, I reached back as if in slow motion, and gently eased my creation into a lazy western headwind. The flashes of setting sun through the trees echoed the contrast of the red wings against the green torso as it left my fingertips toward its encounter with destiny.

An enormous cheer rose from below as the new bird took wing. Quickly the cheer began to fade as the plane stalled, then took a nosedive toward the gravel path below. The vocal support resumed as the craft dipped, then ascended, heading for the evening star that had just made its way into view. A short-lived climb, another stall, then crashing directly into the rocks that formed the border of a trail below.

Destruction. Total destruction. Tiny pieces of balsa wood were strewn throughout the rocks like long toothpicks frozen in jagged false teeth. The only audible sound was the flapping of the ripped tissue against the stone landing strip. Time stood still. Nobody moved or spoke.

I hung from my perch for what seemed like hours. The crowd gradually regained consciousness and quietly meandered back in the general direction of their respective homes. A few of the faithful hung around while I slowly descended the steel ladder of the tower and began to gather up the pieces of my shattered dream. Some followed a few steps behind muttering barely discernable words of dismay mixed with encouragement as I slowly headed for the refuge of home. I was already planning the months it was going to take to reassemble my creation for another test flight.

My mind was suddenly jarred back to the present by a louder than normal scream from across the street. The tiny, tow-headed pilot had managed to guide her craft into a small tree in the corner of her yard with such force and at just the right angle to dislodge the left wing. The wailing was continuous as she rushed on tiptoe with the pieces in her hand to her mother who was rocking on the small front porch.

Within seconds the wing was reattached and the tot returned to the yard to resume her imaginary flights of fancy. Barely ten seconds had lapsed in her frolic and all was back to normal. What a difference fifty years or so make.

Two: **The Swing Set**

I took Adam, my architect intern, to Etowah Elementary School to look at a new playground project. It was a hot, July morning with the sun beating down on us when we met Brad Paulk, the Bartow County grants administrator, and the school principal to discuss the renovation of the playgrounds and the addition of equipment for both the younger and older children. The areas were located on different sides of the school building providing a natural barrier separating the age groups.

On the fourth grade side, among the other pieces of apparatus, there was a set of old-fashioned looking swings. As it turned out, county workers had moved this assembly several years ago from another playground site that had been upgraded.

As we discussed the swing set, someone brought out how dangerous these implements could be to the younger kids, particularly those who might wander into the path of a user and be struck with quite a considerable force. Upon closer inspection I noticed these swings were constructed of much less lethal materials than the ones I remembered from the mill village, and I couldn't help but think of the many hours I had spent in such a device in my childhood.

Even though these swings had some age on them, they were equipped with molded plastic seats that were much lighter than the ones we had in the village. Those were made of wood, probably two by ten material; not the nominal, kiln-dried lumber we see today, but full two-inch thick, dense pine. Each swing was about a foot and a half long with the corners chamfered at forty five degree angles and a large steel eye-bolt on each side that anchored them to chains that supported them from the cross bar above. They were heavy, very heavy, even when not occupied by a ten-year-old body.

The set we had in Atco, on the side of the old school building, consisted of three sections of angled steel supports with three swings centered between each intermediate support for a total of nine swings. At any one time, you were lucky to find five of the nine that were attached at both ends.

The ground below each swing was depressed some eight to ten inches from the constant dragging of bare feet over the years. It seemed that all the rain that fell near the playground ended up in these holes making for great fun splashing through the muddy water with toes pointed downward, forcing a spray of the dirty liquid upward over your entire body.

As with most things in the village, creativity abounded, and most of the available sources of entertainment were used in slightly different ways from those intended. The swings were no exception. Of course we did, on occasion, use them as they were designed to be used and would pump up as high as we could then coast to a slow stop. But that got a bit boring when you had little else to do in the spring and the fall when the pool was closed.

We soon discovered that by standing up in the swing and exhibiting the same pumping motion, we could far exceed the heights we could attain by simply sitting and moving our bodies back and forth. This standing posture was more dangerous, especially when you tried to sit in mid flight. Many a time the swinger would crash to the gravel tarmac while trying to negotiate this delicate transition.

If you pumped hard enough, you reached that point at which slack was created in the ·chain and you experienced a jerk that started your adrenaline flowing. Taken further, this jerk would eventually throw you into an uncontrollable series of gyrations that endangered the adjacent swing chains causing a series of interactions leading to certain disaster. This was especially true if some innocent five-year-old occupied the swing on either side.

The game became seeing how much slack you could create while still maintaining control, then carefully switching to the sitting position so you could bail out. This bail out maneuver meant leaving the swing at the forward high point and seeing how far you could fly through the air with no assistance from the swing that supported you.

Bailing out became a game in and of itself, and lines were drawn in the gravel to show your greatest effort. Exiting the contraption at just the right moment of height and velocity allowed you to fly past the current record mark that disappeared with each summer rain.

Beyond the competition phase, we entered the imagination stage. We tried different types of scarves and capes to pretend we were Superman or Captain Marvel letting our garb trail behind us as we made our leap. This took on a more artistic flavor than the pure athletic endeavor of seeing who could reach the maximum distance. We had no judges awarding points, but we all knew where our own personal leaps ranked in the competition.

However, there were dangers. Once your body left the heavy frame of the swing, the seat would careen wildly back and forth in approximately the same path you had guided it, and it could easily strike you in the back of the head as you stood proudly claiming your new position on terra firma. Many a contestant fled toward home with blood streaming from a gash inflicted by the recently freed object of his rise to fame.

Another activity we participated in on the swing set at the playground was the spin. While sitting still in the swing, you could use your bare feet to spin around and around, winding the chain of the swing tightly above your head. When released, the seat would rotate slowly at first; then faster, and finally go so fast you could hardly see the surroundings as their images sped past.

After slowing to a stop, the swing would begin to circle in the opposite direction and repeat this pattern until gravity finally extracted all the potential energy stored in the chains. When it came to a full stop, you couldn't walk or run in a straight line if your life depended on it. And sometimes it did.

Combining this rotating action with bailing out at high altitudes added a twist, to put it literally, to the game that had evolved. This didn't last long because the dizzy participants usually ended up stumbling back into the path of the reciprocating swing with very negative results.

The playground swings were a great distraction for years, but the real dream came true when my next door neighbor, Boyce, and his brothers, Robert and Billy, got their own swing set and located it between our houses. This was the coup-de-grace. We had our own "Jungle Gym", as they called it back in those days, and it was a real beauty.

In the middle was a ladder that went from the ground to the top of the mechanism flanked by a swing on each side. These were much lighter than the "real" swings at the playground, but they were ours. At least they were theirs, and I was welcome to play on them at any time, unless Boyce got mad at me and chased me around the house to the back door. He could beat me up any time he wanted, but I was faster than he was, so the friendship worked out nicely.

On one end beyond the A-frame support of the unit was a pair of rings, or monkey rings as we called them, and the other end sported a trapeze bar. There was a slide that led down from the ladder in the center, and the whole thing was painted fire engine red. What a beauty it was to behold, and right there in my… well, at least half in my yard.

It wasn't as high as the swings in the playground, but it presented its own set of challenges. The last rung of the ladder was left out to provide access to the sliding board, which made a great place to do a flip as part of a continuous approach to the top of the slide; hardly what the designers had in mind.

You could also hang upside down with your feet locked into the top rung while holding on with your hands to a middle step of the ladder and flip over backward in free fall to the ground, trying to land in a standing position much like a gymnast's dismount in today's meets.

Boyce learned rather quickly that the swings had a lower limit of slack chain tolerance than the playground set, and he regularly was able to lift the legs of the triangular frame off the ground with his high pumps. He finally succeeded in turning the whole assembly over a couple of times, the main top beam narrowly missing his head. This prompted his dad, Ray, to embed the base of the supports in concrete.

Not to be deterred, Boyce quickly found other ways to test the limits of "Mr. Gym". On a dare, which he had a great deal of trouble backing away from, he negotiated the ladder in the center of the system and slowly stood up on the very top with both hands spread wide to achieve balance.

He then walked, tightrope style, sliding each foot a few inches at a time, across the upper support pipe toward the monkey rings at the end of the set. He met his first obstacle at the through-bolt that held one chain of the swing below. Easing his back foot forward to the heel of his front foot he gently stepped over the impediment, pausing briefly to regain his composure. He repeated this process patiently until he was perched above the rings at the end of the top member.

As he made the turn-around to repeat the dare in the other direction, his feet slipped to each side of the cylindrical main beam and he straddled the bar with a muffled thud, which was almost inaudible above the howl he uttered. He then proceeded to flip around, his head clanging into the steel rings before crashing, head first, to the ground below.

As was protocol in the village when someone was hurt or in trouble, I ran, as fast as I could for the safety of the house and peered out the window to see him in a painful tuck on the grass. I left the window to find Mama to see if she had a chore for me to do and let Nature take care of my fallen companion. The Nature I refer to in this case was Irma, Boyce's mother, who was a registered nurse and the one that took care of us in times of medical or disciplinary needs.

We spent many more hours on "our" play set including skinning-the-cat on the trapeze bar and multiple-person slide experiments; but I don't remember Boyce ever venturing to the top bar again to prove his prowess. He did, however, introduce the bailing-out-standing-up maneuver that I never was able to master for fear of certain pain and possible death. Boyce had a lot more daredevil in him than I, which he exhibited on what we referred to as "the trails," but that is another story.

Three: **Nancy Creek**

The last Saturday before Jane started back to work as a middle school counselor was hot, but there was a substantial breeze that made the afternoon almost pleasant. I had promised her a tour of Atco ever since I started writing stories about my upbringing there. After cruising down several streets pointing out where various friends had lived and a few events had taken place, we left the village through the back road off Vigilant Street and turned left onto Gilliam Springs Road.

We passed the baseball complex on the left that had hosted cotton fields during my days in the village. At the time it was a great thrill to walk over and watch the double winged aircraft dust the bowl-laden plants with DDT. We would crouch down at the edge of the field in the plane's path and try to touch it as it zoomed over our heads. Little did we know that the powder being released on us would later be banned.

Just past the vacant diamonds, we turned into the complex and took a right toward the big parking lot down near Nancy Creek, which was the setting for many of my childhood adventures. As we got out of the car I told Jane we were standing approximately where Mr. Cox's barn had been when we did our snake catching at the creek. He also had a beautiful, big, white farmhouse in front of the barn with a large porch that ran around three sides of the two-story frame structure.

Our normal path from the village to the creek lay behind his farm across a strip of meadow, then into a stand of small pine trees that stretched over the hill to the edge of the water. We rarely crossed his pasture because he had a number of curious cows and a big bull that was intent on protecting his territory.

In most places the creek is about twenty feet wide and shallow enough to see the bottom. The water was very clear back then and you could see a variety of colorful rocks and shells that lined its bed. Up stream, the creek ran under a bridge, which separated our hunting territory from Wingfoot Park, which hosted picnics, creek baptisms, and other outdoor activities.

I got hooked on snake hunting the first time I was invited to go to the creek with my neighbor, Jackie Cumbee, and his friend, Cliff Dyar, whom he had known when they both lived in the Goodyear village in Rockmart. Cliff would soon become my main snake catching buddy. Jackie had a large king snake that he kept in his coalhouse that I had the opportunity to meet a week earlier. I was completely taken by the exotic grace exhibited by this beautiful creature that helped me dispel my lifelong fear of snakes, but that is another story.

The purpose of these excursions to Nancy Creek was to catch a meal for Jackie's captive, which fed on other snakes in addition to rats, mice, moles, and birds. The standard menu consisted of what were called queen snakes back then, no relation to king snakes. If anything, they were the opposite of king snakes. They were nasty; a solid greenish brown with a dingy yellow belly. They also had a habit of secreting a smelly substance from musk glands when captured giving rise to our nickname for them – which I had rather not mention.

Queen snakes were numerous along the banks of the creek and they would lie sunning in the branches of low trees and bushes that overhung the water. Upon spotting one, the idea was to slowly creep up from behind and grab it, with gloved hand, before it dropped into the stream and disappeared. Cliff and I worked out several techniques that improved our success rate. We developed a whistle code and hand signals that allowed us to alert the other of the presence of a specimen as we ventured down opposite sides of the creek.

Our capture percentage improved a bit when we discovered that approaching our quarry from the creek side allowed us to avoid reaching through the bushes, which usually spooked the sleeper. This entailed one of us wading slowly up the middle of the creek until a snake was spotted. We used the same whistle signals that we worked out previously, but the person in the water made the slow approach and eventual grab.

On several occasions we allowed a friend to accompany us on our ventures to prove to them that our snake tales were in fact true. We suggested that the visitor wade with one of us up the middle of the creek to get the full effect of the hunt. Their inexperience at creek navigation generally created a significant disturbance, and the queen snakes would start falling out of the trees into the water all around us. At this point our guest's anticipation usually gave way to panic, and he would scramble up the bank heading back to the village in a dead run sloshing all the way home.

We tried a number of techniques over time including the method described in a book I saw at the library by the famous herpetologist, Raymond L. Ditmars. It involved threading a string or small rope through a series of eyes on a long pole forming a loop at the end, then slipping the string around the neck of a sunning specimen. This proved much too cumbersome as the cord was constantly getting tangled in the bushes.

A neighbor in the village suggested a far better method. It was so simple we laughed when we first heard it. There was no way it could work. We were wrong. It turned out to be the most successful capture tool we ever used and our success rate increased significantly.

First you take an old cane-fishing pole and tie a two-foot piece of string to the end of it. Make a simple slipknot in the end of the string about two inches in diameter that would tighten when placed around the neck of the branch dweller and yanked. The weight of the snake was just enough to hold the noose firm but did not harm the catch. It could then be pulled to the bank where a gloved hand would escort it into a waiting catch bag.

As one tried to place the ring around the neck of the unsuspecting serpent from a distance, the animal did not sense a warm body near it. This made our job a lot easier catching the lowly queen snakes, so we ventured to the next level of challenge at Nancy Creek, the common.

I never understood where the name common water snake came from since they were much more rare than the queen snake, but that is what the snake books of the fifties called them. I have seen them referred to as brown water snakes in current texts, but we just called them commons.

Not only were they scarcer at the creek than the queen snake; they were much prettier, and a lot harder to catch. In contrast to the dull, greenish-brown of the queen, this specimen sported dark, reddish brown splotches symmetrically spaced along the length of their body in stark contrast against a light tan background. They closely resemble the poisonous copperhead that is also prevalent in this area.

The commons did not hang out as much in the trees and shrubs, and the string loop method did not prove successful. They were typically sunning on a low bank or straw mass that had collected on a tree root down near the water. One afternoon, we spotted one of these prizes on a lower tier next to the pasture bank. On his belly Cliff was able to crawl up on his belly closer to it than we had gotten before. I sat right behind him on the bank as he slowly lowered his hand to make the grab.

Hesitating, he whispered in a slow, deliberate tone, "It looks like a copperhead."

Now the gloves we used to grab a queen snake or even a common would protect your fingers from the razor sharp, but small, teeth of a nonpoisonous variety, but would offer little or no protection from the fangs of a copperhead or rattlesnake.

Cliff drew his hand back, reconsidered, reached forward, and again retracted his arm. Indecision reigned, even as I encouraged him to make the grab. After all, it was his hand and not mine. And it was a beautiful specimen, one of the largest commons we had ever run across.

He finally decided that it was not a copperhead and lunged for the prize but a split second too late. The elusive reptile scooted into the water just in front of Cliff's outstretched arm and disappeared. I grabbed Cliff's leg as his lurch had thrown him off balance and he was sliding, head first, toward the chilly water. After the rescue, we uttered a few expletives at missing such an opportunity, but it was not our first miss, and we knew it would not be the last.

Upstream from Mr. Cox's place was Wingfoot Park. This was a beautiful wooded area that belonged to the mill. It had picnic tables, swings, and other amenities that could be used by the residents of the village. It was separated from the Cox farm by Gilliam Springs Road, which crossed Nancy Creek over an old concrete bridge. The ineffective guardrail on each side was made up of a few twisted pieces of thin steel angle iron.

Under the bridge on each side of the creek lay some of the slipperiest mud that has ever been. At least it seemed that way. It was our typical, extremely fine-grained, Georgia red clay in a constant state of semi-wetness. The sun never reached the ground under the concrete structure, and the creek water seemed to leach into the clay bank by osmosis.

On this afternoon, Jane and I ventured off the walking trail to the foot of the bridge, and I examined the familiar mud flat below it. From my angle it didn't seem to be that wet, so I decided to ease across under the road to let Jane see what remained of the once beautiful park.

I reached my right hand out to the bridge abutment and eased my way onto the reddish gray surface. It seemed to hold, so I took a few more baby steps forward. Just as I turned to signal Jane to follow, my left tennis shoe began to slip. I tried to steady myself with my right foot, but it too started toward the water six feet away and closing.

I took four or five quick back steps as my rear headed toward the ground. I hit with a slosh in the near liquid mass that was just below the visible surface. As I recovered from the concussion of hitting the ground, I quickly realized that I was slowly sliding down the bank toward the creek. Dragging my hands and digging in my heels proved fruitless and I felt my velocity slowly increase as the slope of the bank gradually began to sharpen.

Worse yet, the vee formed by my legs made an efficient plow that began scooping the loose mire into my shorts as I progressed down the slope. By the time I hit the cold water I had accumulated a substantial load of silt in my pants that had made its way up my … well, as far as it could go.

I sat stunned in the two-foot deep section of the branch and suddenly became aware of my lovely wife, Jane, who was bent over double with laughter on the bank behind me. All I could do was splash a little water in her direction to relieve my frustration before I, too, burst into laughter.

Luckily, there were no games in progress at the ball fields and the walking trail was empty. I struggled to my feet. After seeing the coast was clear, I dropped my pants into the flowing stream to wash the grimy mess from my shorts and my body. I am sure I was quite a sight standing in the creek with my pants around my knees, sloshing a hand full of water at a time between my legs and into my mud stained clothing.

After the cleansing ritual, I waded down stream to a point where some rocks made exiting the creek possible without further embarrassing incident. On the way to the minivan Jane tried to offer comforting words between snickers, but for some reason they didn't seem very sincere.

Jane drove my minivan back to the house while I straddled the rear seat in a semi-kneeling position to keep from staining my surroundings with the residual deposits still clinging to and inside of my outer and inner garments.

I have not taken Jane back to the creek since that late summer afternoon, and she will just have to wait a while before I take her back to see Wingfoot Park.

Four. **The Company Store**

The early spring sky was overcast as we made our way around the large open field where the City of Euharlee hosts an annual powwow. The gathering is held each October and draws a large group of Native American attendees and visitors from a wide area of the country. It offers opportunities to learn about the history and traditions of the Cherokees who cultivated the land and fished the rivers here many years ago.

I was asked by the city's civil engineer to contact the city manager, Frankie Harris, and set up a time to visit with her and several city council members to discuss some enhancements to the park and facilities they were planning to add. A small model with the proposed placement of the buildings was on display at City Hall.

After passing around several ideas about the layout we walked over to look at the site. It was a large open field encircled by low pine trees and sloped gently upward away from the parking area. At the top of the open area the incline reversed and dropped down toward Euharlee Creek, which was hidden by a thick stand of undergrowth.

Stakes with blue ribbons attached to the top marked the suggested corners of various structures and activities. We talked about locations and how they related to other facilities, the creek, and the large circle in the center of the field around which the main activities would take place. A few ideas were tossed around about possible amenities that would help make the park attractive to the city residents throughout the year.

As we headed back to City Hall, I struck up a conversation with Frankie who grew up in the Atco Mill Village during the same period that I did. At almost the same time, we both brought up the fact that nobody locked their doors back then. It was something you just never thought of and had no need to do. I only remember ours being locked during a vacation we took for a full two weeks to St. Augustine, Florida, but that is another story.

As kids we would wander in and out of our friends' houses like the entire village was our home and we were just circulating from one living area to the other. If you misbehaved while in someone else's house, you were just as likely to get a spanking there as you were at home. And our parents were very satisfied with that arrangement.

It seemed that almost everybody in the Atco Village had a nickname – at least all the boys that I can remember did. They were addressed as Nougie, Hoss, Monk, Silo and Cotton to mention a few. Moose, Bookey, Pod, Satch, Fireball, and Woody could also be heard around the hamlet.

Fruit Jackson was a bit older than I was, but he was one of my best buddies in the early days in the village. I was at his house when I got a call from Sister telling me that I had a new brother, and his name was David. I wanted to name him Charles, which was Fruit's real name, but Mama and Daddy had already decided to call him David Hayne.

Another group of monikers I remember related to a couple of pieces of luggage. The oldest brother was named Suitcase, and the younger was known as Satchel. I often wondered if a third brother would have been called Briefcase.

Other names like Fuzz, Prune, and Catfish flash though my memory along with their youngest sibling simply referred to as "Little". Apparently when nicknames ran short, the next in line would be called "Little".

I have been asked on a number of occasions what my nickname was during my tenure in the village. I only remember a few of them: "Haig-leg" and "Little Haigler" were most common followed by "Haig and Haig". I did not find out until I went to Georgia Tech that Haig and Haig was the name of an expensive brand of scotch whiskey and a very good one at that. At least that is what some of my fraternity brothers told me.

The other nickname that has apparently passed the test of time is "The Haig". This blossomed during my college days and has seemed to keep its grip on me until this day. I did learn in architecture school that "The Hague", pronounced the same way, is the seat of government of the Netherlands, known to most of us as Holland.

One of the things I remember about growing up in the village is that very few things were not shared. If you bought a sucker or Popsicle it was expected that you let those you were with have a lick or two. The same was true with a Coke or a cup of ice cream you ate with a wooden spoon. I did not smoke then but those who did would call "ducks" when someone else lit up, and that allowed them to take the last puff on the Camel or Lucky Strike.

These various treats could be purchased at the village store located on Goodyear Avenue across from the mill. We lived in the first house past the store so it was very easy for us to get to, and most everybody heading there walked down the sidewalk in front of our house. Our front porch was a great vantage point from which to observe the majority of the goings-on in the hub of the village.

On beyond the store from our house, a pair of train tracks crossed the divided entrance road to the village. One of these spurs led into the mill area and was used to transport raw materials and finished goods into and out of the village. The second curved toward Cassville Road and led to the small trestle where I spent many hours fishing.

Both tracks ran through the sidewalk and planted divider between the two traffic lanes. This intersection always fascinated me, and I enjoyed pulling my wagon across the tracks at the sidewalk. I loved to watch the black, solid rubber wheels travel over the rails and bump across the grooves made by the flanges on the inside of the big steel wheels.

The train that traversed this siding generally was just a small switch engine with maybe five or six cars. Since it ran very seldom it was a real treat to be able to get to the tracks in time to watch the train make the crossing. The piercing whistle, roar of the engine, squeaking wheels, diesel exhaust smell, and vibrating ground created an experience that stimulated all the senses.

One of the engineers that worked on this siding was Pete McDaniel. He was a friend of the family, and on one occasion while I was watching the train pass, he stopped the engine on a section of track a good ways away from the mill. He leaned out of the cab and motioned for me to come up the engine steps. My heart stopped for a moment, and I took a deep breath as the meaning of this gesture registered in my stunned young mind.

For a moment my feet refused to move and seemed to have grown roots to keep me safely attached to the ground. Finally I broke free and scampered up the steel stairs and grabbed his outstretched hand. As he pulled me into the cab I gasped at the size and number of dials and gizmos in front of me. Just above my head a wooden handle was suspended on a rope hanging from the ceiling.

He picked me up toward the cord and said, "Pull it."

With a bit of hesitation I reached cautiously for the dangling wood cylinder. When I took it in my hand I began to squeeze until my knuckles turned white.

"Go ahead, pull it," he repeated with a higher degree of authority in his voice.

I closed my eyes and yanked as hard as I could. The cab was instantly filled with a near deafening sound that echoed through the iron enclosure. I let go of the whistle rope instantly as a rush of adrenaline surged through my trembling body. I jumped down the steps and headed across an area of asphalt to the back door of the store that opened into the basement.

This lower level held my favorite part of the store. It was the grill that was operated for years by "Mac". He could cook up anything you wanted, but for us to actually get to eat there was a very rare treat. You could, however, when you had a nickel or two, buy a Coke or an RC and a pack of peanuts to pour in the bottle. If you asked for the bottle cap, you could carefully pry out the cork liner and stick it on the front of your tee shirt and wear it like a medal, the cork holding it in place from the inside.

The front of the store had a large triangular recess in the corner forming a covered porch with entrance doors on each side. The tiny Atco Post Office was nestled between these portals and was defined by post office boxes on each side and what was essentially a wire cage above. My aunt, whom everyone called Sister, worked there for many years under the supervision of the Atco postmaster, Bessie Sue Smith. My little brother, David, with his way with words, always called her "Sessie-Boo."

We moved to town about the time they closed the Atco Post Office. Sister was transferred and went to work as the first female employee of the Cartersville Post Office. She was not welcomed at first, but eventually she became just one of the guys.

The inside of the store was bathed with natural light streaming through the set of clerestory windows that ran the length of the heavy timber structure. These high windows could be opened and closed by a long crank assembly. This allowed for ventilation in the summer since air conditioning was still many years in the future.

A variety of dry goods was available at the store as well as a large, adequately stocked grocery section. Few toys were on display except around Christmas, but in early spring, kites and kite cord were readily available for a quarter.

The store had almost anything you really needed. Even bubble gum could be bought for a penny from the little globe-topped machines at the store entrance. They each were stocked with tempting "prizes" spread around against the glass. You were the lucky one if you happened by the machine when it was almost empty because the prizes that were so cherished were all stacked up near the bottom.

One day when I was about five years old, I walked home from the store and handed Mama a twenty-dollar bill. Now, twenty dollars back then was easily equal to a hundred today. Her mouth dropped open and she half spoke, half screamed, "Where did you get that?"

"At the store," I told her, and she began to grill me on exactly what the circumstances were that caused this money to come into my possession.

When banks cancelled checks back then, they had machines that punched a bunch of tiny holes in them before they returned them to you in your bank statement. Sometimes I would get to play with the cancelled checks, and I was fascinated by these minute punctures. I could line them up with the holes in other checks and see through them.

Apparently on this particular afternoon, I had decided to take one of these perforated checks down and give it to Libby at the store as I had seen Mama do on many occasions. Libby worked down at the store that her husband, Roberts Bradford managed for a number of years.

The Bradfords were long time friends with my folks and Libby saw nothing wrong with my cashing a check for Mama. She just did not happen to notice that the check had all those tiny holes signifying that it had already served its purpose.

Once the truth came out, I was marched straight to the store to give the twenty dollars back to Libby who was still unaware of the errant transaction. She dug out the check and returned it to me, and I handed it over to my mother standing beside me. I learned the lesson that day that money can get you into trouble.

It was a sad day when the store building joined the old school, barbershop, and swimming pool falling victim to the wrecking ball. It, along with the other discarded structures, housed many memories for several generations and represented an era that is slowly fading from our collective consciousness.

Five: **The King and I**

It was a dry, hot August afternoon in the third year of a drought that made your mouth feel like you had a ball of cotton in it. I had taken my stepson John by to pick up Alan in Dalton where he was living at the time, and driven out to a golf course we had never played near Chatsworth.

We were having our usual rounds, more in the woods than out, when we teed off at the twelfth hole. It was a three par that was all water, a small lake with no fairway between the tee and the green. The designers of golf courses have figured out a way to insert a giant magnet into water hazards, and all three of us fell victim to its mighty force.

The two boys, as usual, scooted out ahead of me around the pond while I was trying to keep up in my cart. As I rounded the first turn I caught sight of a familiar shape in a stand of pine trees a ways off the path. I jumped out of the cart and instinctively grabbed for my putter.

There next to a small pile of limbs, was a beautiful Eastern king snake. It must have just shed its skin, because the sunrays that fell on him made the yellow chain design on his black body look like gold on a velvet cloth. He was incredibly beautiful with not a single blemish anywhere on his luminescent scales.

At first he was unaware of my presence as I stood absorbing the beauty of his lazy motion toward the brush pile. Only when I reached down and picked him up at mid-body did he acknowledge his stalker and begin his escape attempts.

The first grab was too close to his head, and he turned to inflict pain to my bare hand. I had a thin golf glove on my left, which offered some protection, but I had instinctively reacted with my right. I dropped him immediately, and he scurried for the brush as I grabbed again. He struck once more, and I dropped him again only to have him go for my bare ankles.

I danced around the pine bow heap, alternating between grabbing, dropping, and jumping clear of the strike zone. I could hear the boys all the way across the lake laughing at my antics and it must have looked like something between a Zulu war dance and the Teaberry Shuffle.

I finally latched onto the serpent far enough away from his business end for him not to reach my hand or body in his numerous attempts to snag me. As he calmed down, I walked back over to the cart and headed around the water holding the king snake at arm's length in my gloved hand.

I arrived at the green where the boys were still in hysterics at my impromptu ballet. They got over that real quick as I chased each one in turn around the drop area near the green. When we slowed down, they petted this marvelous creature for a minute. Then I took him up the hill behind the green and set him free. For a minute he lay there looking at me as if we had some sort of bond, then he slowly headed up the hill and disappeared into the pine straw.

As we continued our futile round of golf, I recalled my first up close and personal encounter with a king snake or any snake for that matter. It belonged to a neighbor, Jackie Cumbee, who lived two houses up my street in the Atco village. I had just finished the sixth grade, and he was already in the tenth.

Before I go any further, let me stress the fact that I was brought up with a deathly fear of snakes passed on to me by my mother. In my very early school years, I went fishing almost every day at the trestle over Pettit Creek. My fear of this slithery reptile was so intense that I dreaded warm weather coming because it brought them out of hibernation.

Daddy was the scoutmaster of Troop 15 in the mill village and told me about Jackie bringing his snake to one of their meetings to show it off to the other scouts. He encouraged me to go up the street and meet Jackie and get him to show me his pet. He knew that I had inherited Mama's immense fear of snakes and thought this could help me overcome it.

It took a few days to get up my nerve, but finally I made the trek up Goodyear Avenue to the corner and up the walk to Jackie's house. His mother, Hilda, came to the door and told me that Jackie was out in the coalhouse with his snake. The coalhouses in Atco were exactly that, where coal was delivered and kept until some poor, snotty nosed eight-year-old like me toted it to the main house in oblong buckets we called scuttles.

Until natural gas was run to the village in the mid fifties, our main source of heat was a large, coal burning stove in the living room supplemented by coal fireplaces in each bedroom. We had a small electric heater in the kitchen and an even smaller one in the bathroom. It was my job to bring in four scuttles of coal each day, which I hated doing and usually postponed until well after dark. The coalhouse was a very scary place at night and the trek was always very cold.

As I slowly descended the eight concrete steps from Jackie's porch to the walk, my mind was racing with great anticipation. As I realized this reaction was due primarily to fear, I took an immediate left and ran through the front yard toward my house. As I crossed the walk of the intervening house, I remembered that Daddy was at home and he knew where I was going. This would mean a bit of heckling if I told him I had chickened out on my way to seeing the snake.

I gathered my courage and turned left and walked between our house and the house that Boyce, my best friend, had vacated in early summer when his family moved to Decatur, Alabama where his dad, Ray, had been promoted to plant manager. It had nearly killed me to see him leave as he had been as near a twin as one could have and not be related.

I took a left up the cinder alley behind the empty house and crunched my way up the short rise to the entrance to Jackie's coalhouse. I stepped up to the right onto a small landing that had a closed storeroom door to my left. Without turning my head, I could sense that the door to the main room on my right was open as a cool breeze drifted out over my sweat-laden body.

As I made my cautious turn toward the opening, my pupils began a slow expansion adjusting from the bright sunlight to the darkened interior of the bin. Gradually, the image of a slim figure bending over a large wooden box began to materialize in the dimness below me. His upper body and head were silhouetted against the back wall that was illuminated by rays falling through a small window. The box in front of him had screen wire enclosing all four sides and an open top.

With great trepidation, I stepped down to the bare, red clay floor inside and tapped lightly on the door beside me, half hoping he wouldn't hear it. I could feel my heart pulsating in my temples and my shaky nerve was fading fast.

He slowly turned toward me with both his hands outstretched and revealed the object of his attention, and the quarry I had come to witness. There, right in front of me, draped between his hands and entwined in his fingers, was a six-foot long, Eastern king snake. The entire scene played out in slow motion like in the movies when the director is attempting to make a lasting impression on the audience. As Jackie's body came to a halt, the flowing black and yellow form draped between his arms slowly turned its head and looked straight at me.

As my anxious brain became fully aware of what lay only a few feet from my young body, I grabbed both sides of the doorframe behind me in an effort to resist the adrenaline rush that was loudly screaming, "Run! Run, you fool!"

I know my eyes were as big as silver dollars as my host softly said, "Hi there."

A muffled "Heh" was the only sound my lungs could force through my frozen countenance, as I continued to maintain my death grip on the doorframe. My eyes were fixed on the head of this sleek animal and I was mesmerized by the forked tongue that was flicking out at me as if to say, "Hello there, stranger."

The next words out of the mouth of this mild mannered young man echoed through the canyons of my mind like a nearby clap of thunder. "Do you want to hold it?" he said softly, stepping toward me with his hands outstretched.

"Hold it? Hold it! What do you mean, Hold It? Are you crazy? Hold it!" The words kept clamoring around in my head; and again, it was all I could do to resist the urge to flee and never venture back to this scary place.

After several deep breaths and some encouraging words from the owner of this majestic beast, I nodded and slowly extended my hands in his direction. He walked toward me, gently lowered the elegant form onto my open hands, and said, "Move slowly and don't grip him too tight, and everything will be all right."

The slender body felt cool as Jackie placed it in my trembling hands, and I could feel its muscles begin to constrict and grip my fingers. It was not at all slimy, unlike what I had heard about this animal. Waves of excitement surged through my skinny frame as this king slowly eased forward in my hand and started to crawl up my left wrist. It took all my focus to resist the temptation to sling this creature back to my host and run like hell.

After a few minutes, during which time I probably set a record for breath holding, Jackie reached forward and the elegant creature slowly made its way back into his hands and then back into its temporary abode. I walked over and peered into the cage to see the critter glide gracefully through the pine straw and around the rocks and short limbs that had been selected to create a more natural habitat.

From that moment on I was hooked. I was totally fascinated by this animal that had, for years, been the object of one of my greatest fears.

King snakes are great. They, along with a number of other species like rat snakes and chicken snakes, are constrictors. They are not poisonous, but kill their prey by striking and holding it with their teeth then wrapping their body around it and squeezing the life out of it. Constrictors are much easier to tame and make better pets than water snakes, black racers, and the large variety of garden and ground snakes.

Some time later, my new friend Jackie introduced me to Cliff Dyar who had just moved to the village. His dad was transferred from the Goodyear Plant in Rockmart as was Jackie's, and they had been buddies there. A few days later I was invited to accompany them over to Nancy Creek, which ran down the west side of the village. The purpose of this excursion was to catch a couple of water snakes for Jackie's king snake's dinner.

My encounter with the king snake and the trip to the creek started me on a snake-hunting journey that I still enjoy today. Cliff and I became great buddies and spent countless hours tromping through woods, turning over rocks, wading creeks, and riding the back roads in search of this elusive creature. Some of these adventures turned out to be a bit harrowing, but I managed to survive them with many memories and fodder for numerous other stories.

Six: **Fishing Rodeo**

The second job inspection of the day took me out Sugar Valley Road to the new Bartow County Fire Station site on a hot and humid August morning. The sweat induced by the clammy heat of the fieldwork had almost dried on my forehead as I sat at the stoplight at Burnt Hickory Road on the way back into town.

Down the small hill just ahead of me I could see the railroad crossing that had been carved through the once beautiful Wingfoot Park to sate the ever-growing appetite of the huge, coal burning power plant west of town.

Just past the tracks was the old bridge over Nancy Creek where Cliff Dyar and I spent many hours snake hunting. A wide clearing cut across the creek on the right side where a sewer line was installed recently. It completely obliterated the habitat where most of our snake gathering adventures had taken place.

The baseball complex on the right was a huge cotton field when I was growing up in the village. It was great fun to go over when we heard the double-winged crop duster planes spreading their loads of DDT. We would run to the end of the field and duck down behind a hedgerow to see how close we could get to the swooping craft. Why we didn't all die a long time ago from exposure to this toxin is beyond me.

To the left on what was Mr. Cox's pasture is a new housing development, aptly named Wingfoot Park. A bunch of cows and a mean bull occupied this field when I lived in Atco, and we were all chased more than once as we tried to take the short cut to the upper part of the creek.

Perhaps the most memorable feature of this pasture was the, ahem... ditch. It ran from the northern area of the village to Nancy Creek and deposited its, uh, burden into the creek near the bridge. I think the politically correct term these days is effluent for what flowed through our famous ditch, but if it looks like a rose and smells like a rose, it probably – well you get the point.

I would like to stress that this was downstream from the site where the baptisms took place up near the picnic area. Jumping this chasm was a popular sport among us young daredevils, but that will not be addressed here.

I turned right at the top of the hill that was once known as "Boss Row" into the backside of the village onto Mayflower Street. I turned left on Goodyear Avenue and drove past the tennis courts where my house once stood. After passing the mill, the old store site, and the clubhouse, I crossed the old pair of train tracks.

The spur on the right that ran parallel to Cassville Road has been removed, and the old bed is now a grassed trail with small pines serving as a border. This track once led across the small trestle over Pettit Creek where I spent a large portion of my young life. An attractive serpentine wooden walking bridge that connects the village to town has replaced it.

As a small child I walked to this trestle every day that weather, and Mama, permitted and spent hours fishing in the creek for whatever might be tempted by my bait, which usually consisted of something I dug up in the yard or a grasshopper or cricket that I was able to corral.

At some point we discovered another enticement that was especially attractive to the small bream, which were the usual catch from the trestle. Wasp larvae. These were little white worms with red heads that incubate in the small cylinders inside a wasp's nest, which was generally referred to as "wauss ness" in the mill village.

Securing this new form of appealing bait could be an exciting adventure in and of itself. In warm weather, the nests were plentiful around Atco and could usually be found hanging from the gable or the soffits of the coalhouses that were positioned behind each house. The larger the nest the better, but the level of danger also increased as more wasp guards would be stationed around these choice discoveries.

The idea was to align the longest cane pole you had with the nest while peeking from behind a corner, trying not to alert the sentinels. A quick jab at just the right spot would send the nest drifting to the ground amid a cloud of angry, buzzing stingers that scattered in all directions searching for the interloper.

You didn't stick around to see if the attempt had been successful. The key was to run as fast as you could away from the furor you had created. After awhile you could sneak back around from the other direction to see if you had accomplished your mission. One swift sprint-and-grab secured the newly plucked treasure, and you were in business. A small paper sack served as a bait box for the nest as you picked up your pole and headed down the track to the creek.

The tracks over the trestle were attached to crossties, which were supported by several eighteen-inch deep beams that ran in the direction of the track. The beams rested on deep girders about two feet wide that were spaced about twelve feet apart and jutted out from the side of the trestle some three feet. About twelve feet above the water, these girders made a perfect place to sit while tempting the fish with this new treat.

Extreme caution had to be exercised as you opened the bag because there was a good chance that one or more of the fledgling wasps had hatched from its group cocoon. Sitting on the low girder was a little bit precarious and was made even more so when one of the little critters emerged undetected, only to be discovered crawling up your pants leg.

I inherited the love of fishing from my granddaddy on my mother's side. His name was Frank Claude Watkins, Jr. but we all just called him "Papa". He could fish from dawn to dark without a nibble and never get discouraged. He and my uncle Gene, who lived with him in Acworth, even raised their own bait, but that is another story.

Papa loved to fish for anything. Even carp. He didn't eat them, but a five-pounder would really put up a fight and was great fun to catch. These scavengers feed off the bottom and basically will eat anything, but they especially like fish eggs so we were told. Well, I guess the thing that looks the most like fish eggs is a dough ball.

Now my mother has claimed for years that her granddaddy, Frank Claude senior, invented this special concoction, made in the kitchen with flour, water and several secret ingredients, one of which is cotton. It must be virgin cotton from the stalk and not the kind you buy in the store, because that smells like medicine; and carp, just like kids, don't like medicine.

Anyway, Papa shared his recipe with me, including some stinky cheese to improve the aroma, and a few other things I can't quite recall. I got Mama to help me cook up a batch so I could take it to the upcoming fishing rodeo.

These events were sponsored by Goodyear and were held periodically at different venues. They were open to village kids of all ages. Awards were presented for catching the biggest fish and other criteria for each age group, and I was out for the grand prize. The upcoming rodeo was to be held at Allatoona Landing, and Papa had caught many a big carp from this dock.

I had my secret formula in my pocket as I climbed into the school bus early Saturday morning in back of the Atco store for the trip to the lake. As others boarded, I noticed that nobody would sit by me. Even my good buddies would pause briefly in front of my seat and then head on back down the aisle. It took a minute, but I finally figured out it was the cheese flavoring in the dough ball mix that had dimmed my popularity significantly.

Reaching our destination, we streamed out of the bus down the hill, like ants headed for the honey pot, to the floating dock that stuck out a hundred or so feet into the lake. Allatoona Dam was built across the Etowah River in the late forties primarily as a flood control reservoir to detain the spring runoff and abate the flooding that occurred at regular intervals downstream from Cartersville. For years this had been a problem, especially in Rome where the Etowah joins up with the Oostanaula to form the Coosa River flowing on into Alabama.

In winter, water is released to make room for the spring rains causing the lake level to vary some forty feet from summer to winter, and all the docks are built to rise and fall with the water surface. Back then most were constructed of treated wood mounted over empty fifty-five gallon drums for buoyancy. Every time a boat passed, the wake would rock the assembly and the barrels would bang together scaring every fish for miles around.

We spread out along the narrow pier and dropped our gear into the murky waters. I had my can of worms that I'd dug up from the soft ground in back of our house, which I baited up with first; I was saving my secret weapon for later in the day.

Well, to put it bluntly, the fish were just not biting. By noon, only a few tiny bream and a small catfish had been taken, none by me. I ate my Vienna sausage and soda crackers after washing the "worm" off my hands in the lake water.

After lunch, I figured I had given the carp enough freedom, and it was time to show this bunch how a real fisherman could bring home the bacon, so to speak. I eased the small, aromatic bag from my front pocket and placed it beside me, making sure it remained hidden from those nearby.

I pulled out a large pinch of the tactile substance and rolled it into a rough spherical shape. I stuck the hook through the mass and lowered the baited snare all the way to the bottom. I held my South Bend fiberglass rod firmly with both hands and waited for the impending strike.

I waited. I waited some more. Nothing was happening. What had gone wrong with the wonder-bait that had never failed Papa? I waited some more then figured something must be amiss. So I slowly reeled the rig in.

As I pulled the hook near me I was shocked to see that the dough had apparently dissolved and all that was left on the hook was a soggy wad of cotton. What had gone wrong? My secret weapon had let me down.

Not to be deterred, I pulled out another glob of mix and molded it tightly around the hook. For good measure, I stuck an extra active worm on the hook beside the dough ball and let the refurbished snare sink into the muddy water.

The combination worked. Within minutes, the end of the rod began to tremble then suddenly bend into the water. I grabbed the reel and felt a giant tug that almost jerked the rod from my hand. I held on as the line and end of the rod made an erratic lurch to the right. Suddenly, the three entrants on that side grabbed for their lines as their corks sank from sight.

Then my line raced back across to the left, and the two guys beside me got hits on their rods. The six of us flailed away trying to land our catches for what seemed like forever. Other contestants gathered around in disbelief that six people had all hooked a real fighter at the same time.

The excitement quickly waned as all of a sudden each rod flexed back to normal, slack appeared in the lines, and corks bobbed to the surface. I reeled in as fast as I could only to behold a tangle of hooks, line and sinkers that my would-be prize had snagged on his way to gaining freedom.

It took an hour to untangle the mess, and by then it was almost time for the competition to end. I packed up my meager gear and walked to the end of the dock where I pulled the remaining smelly concoction out of the bag. I tossed it in the lake and watched it slowly begin to fade from sight as it drifted toward the bottom.

Just before it disappeared, a huge shape appeared from the depths and grabbed the discarded morsel. He shook his head a couple of times then glanced upward as if to mock me. Then this "Moby Carp" slowly swam away.

Seven: **Blackberries**

Not many people get married on the Fourth of July. After all, it is "Independence Day." Probably even fewer get up on this day, dress in jeans, and spend a large part of the morning picking blackberries in the hot sun, bodies coated with insect repellant, and toting a cutoff plastic, half gallon milk carton on their belt.

This discarded milk jug is trimmed just above the handle in a low arc that severs the original spout and leaves the full girth of the container open to receive the berries. Inserting your belt through the jug handle and placing it just behind your first loop produces, in theory, a handy pouch allowing you to use both hands for picking. In actuality, you end up holding the thorn-laden branches in one hand while swatting bugs and picking with the other.

This day marked our sixteenth year of wedlock, and of the annual trek to the blackberry patches. When we got married, we had four children between us. John, six and Kathryn, eight belonged to Jane; Alan, nine and Michael, twelve were mine. In the family tradition, from that first year, we loaded the whole clan up in the car and headed for the harvest.

For the most part, the kids hated it. The briars, the bugs and spiders, the heat, the weeds, the sweat, the bees; they complained about nearly everything. Their only enjoyment seemed to be the duels with the insect spray and putting the berries down each other's backs and squashing them. Those stains are a bit hard to get out.

When we got home, we had to put all our clothes in the back hall to be washed, since we had certainly traipsed through miles of poison oak and chigger beds. In turn, we took hot showers to rid our bodies of the plant's evil juice and the red bugs before either could infect us. We had to set a timer for five minutes because the antique water heater in our over one-hundred-year-old house could only heat thirty minutes of water at a time. No one could turn on a faucet or flush anything during this period, or the shower occupant would get scalded.

None of the kids have gone with us in the last several years on our annual berry gathering, and this year was no exception. Our usual pasture of plenty was located along the walking trail at Dellinger Park on the outskirts of town. Three years of draught and an increase in hungry walkers had produced slim pickin's over the past few forays to the Park.

Two years ago, we stumbled upon another promising area on a large, north-facing bank in front of the middle school where Jane taught for several years. The school is located in Emerson, and residents there claim it is the Kudzu capital of the world. Power poles, trees, abandoned vehicles, and an occasional napping highway department worker have been known to disappear until the first frost.

Watching the Kudzu grow is the leading pastime in Emerson, but you had better not stand in one place too long. Some of the sculptured images formed by this kinetic plant creeping up guy wires and cascading down between towering pines could rival anything by Rodin or Moore. Some people find figures in the clouds, but the residents of Emerson see them in the Kudzu and watch them change before their eyes.

I mention Kudzu because our newly discovered blackberry haven is being taken over by it. The trick to finding the berries here is to spot a suspicious lump in the Kudzu patch, wade over to it and peal it back to expose the thorny boughs of the berry bushes. Luckily, Kudzu has no briars, but it has three leaves like another species that hangs out around blackberries.

Every time I see a blackberry bush, I think of Rowland Springs and Aunt Beck. Everybody in town knew Aunt Beck Donahoo and most tried to claim her as real kin, which I was; my mother's mother was a Donahoo so I could legitimately call her Aunt Beck, even though she was actually my great aunt.

Rowland Springs and the area around Aunt Beck's had the best blackberries anywhere in the five-county area. The patches were so popular that trails had been worn through them, and you could walk right up to the massive plants and pick half a bucket full without bending over. The bushes rose well over your head and were laden with more berries than you have ever seen. That's the way to pick blackberries.

The Rowland Springs area was once a tourist resort with lodging quarters and dining facilities, but the main attraction was the water. Bubbling out of the ground in seven different areas, the mineral water was said to have all manner of healing capabilities, and people came from far and wide to drink from the springs. Bottles of water were even sold to those wishing to take it home to relatives or for extended treatment of their many ills.

Only three of the springs were accessible back in those picking days when we visited almost every week in the summer. Aunt Beck could pick more blackberries than the rest of us "city folk" put together, and we could hardly keep up with her as she headed up the path to the house carrying a full bucket of this tasty summer fruit. That was when she was eighty. She lived to be a hundred and four, and I am sure that rough, country lifestyle had a lot to do with her longevity.

Memories abound of this wonderful place and began for me at a very early age. In the mid-forties, when my dad was overseas serving in the Army during World War II, Mama and my aunt, Sister, would take me out to Rowland Springs all the time. I loved the country and the attention. Everybody felt sorry for me because my daddy had been sent off to war when I was only seven months old, and I was now pushing three. They spoiled me rotten I guess, but I enjoyed every minute of it, so they say.

On one of those visits, a large rooster that wandered around the place flogged me. Now I'm not exactly sure what flogging means, but it apparently scared the heck out of me and made Aunt Beck furious. The next time we went to see her for dinner, I asked Aunt Beck where that mean old rooster was. She slowly cocked her head toward the large serving bowl in the center of the table, cracked a devious grin of revenge, and winked at me. I never ate chicken and dumplings again.

Those visits were to what would later come to be known as the Big House. It had four large rooms on each of two floors with wide center halls, front columns that went up two stories and a steep pitched roof. Aunt Beck and her two daughters lived there for years until one spring night in the late forties when a tornado swooped down out of the darkness and took off the attic, part of the second floor, and opened the back wall of the kitchen like a big swinging door. I still remember the sight of all those lanterns, pots, pans, and other utensils hanging on the nails in the huge kitchen wall that hinged at one corner and stood ajar at a thirty-degree angle.

After the storm hit, Aunt Beck, Anne, and Louise moved into a much smaller place at the other end of the property, which had no running water and no electricity until the mid-sixties. They had to haul water every day from the springs and used it to cook over a big, wood-burning stove. Aunt Beck could outrun anybody alive from the spring, up the hill to the house, toting two overflowing pails of sparkling water. This cabin is the place I remember visiting for hours on end, sitting out on the narrow screened front porch and listening to the fabulous yarns Aunt Beck could weave.

She told one tale over and over again about the time she got up in the top of a closet to get a blanket down as the fall breezes began to stir. It felt heavier than usual as she let it fall down to the floor and began to unwrap it. She started to hear a buzzing sound that got louder and louder as the bedding unfurled. At the last roll, a large timber rattlesnake tumbled out and coiled to attention with its rattles ablaze. With little to-do, Aunt Beck picked up the twelve-gauge shotgun she kept in the corner and blew its head off, right there in the bedroom.

To the right of the small house was a swing suspended from a low limb of an old oak tree behind the wide, barren area of red clay where visitors parked. Years of foot-dragging had worn away the dirt around a large root below the swing, and you could easily be dumped on your face if you didn't keep your feet up and out of the way when swinging.

Behind the swing there was a bank that sloped down to a flat clearing some fifty feet below. This incline was covered with pine straw from the numerous seedlings that had matured and made a great place to slide, in the absence of snow, which is rare here in the Southeast. The straw was as slick as a baby's butt, and a big piece of cardboard or an old discarded section of metal roof made an excellent sled. There were several small rock outcroppings and numerous pine trees you had to avoid, but otherwise you could enjoy the ride of your life down the pine straw laden course.

At the bottom of the hill, one of the springs lay off to the left. It was the easiest to access and was used for quenching the thirst of the many who had participated in the activities in the hollow over the years. There were several old wooden church pews roughly aligned around what once was a makeshift altar. A large stone barbeque structure was set off to one side and flanked by several aging picnic tables arranged end to end. Outdoor church services had been held here many years earlier, and they were usually followed by a picnic or cookout that would go on all afternoon. I recall many wonderful times in my younger years playing in this valley and surrounding woods.

An adjacent creek provided wading, catching crawfish, and other diversions befitting a growing boy on a hot summer afternoon. Heavy woods lined the other side of the creek, and as kids, we were always told not to venture to the opposite bank. It was too snaky. That bank would later become a favorite venue for Cliff Dyar and me, after snake catching became a hobby.

I remember the time when Nancy, one of Aunt Beck's nieces, was hosting a gathering for her ninetieth birthday and invited me to come and bring my twelve-string guitar. It was in the late sixties, and everyone was heavily into the folk music scene. Nancy had six girls and three boys who were all there along with a large crowd from the neighborhood. It was quite a celebration and lasted late into the evening.

At some point, one of the kids brought me my guitar, and I started to play some up-beat sing-along that everybody knew like "Cotton Fields." Everybody started singing. We were really getting into it when, all of a sudden, Aunt Beck started to dance. Not just dance, but Buck Dance. If you have never seen a ninety-year-old buck dance, you have truly missed out on one of life's great pleasures. Soon the whole crowd was dancing. If the neighbors had not been party to the shindig, I am sure the authorities would have been summoned.

As I spread the Pet-Ritz piecrust over my annual blackberry cobbler attempt, I told Jane about the most vivid memory I have of Aunt Beck. At a family reunion at Thelma's, when Aunt Beck was ninety-eight, I eased back into the kitchen after most of the crowd had headed home. There was Aunt Beck, leaning back in her chair, her feet propped on the table, swigging a "tall-boy" Schlitz – straight out of the can.

Eight: **Beach Beach Beach**

Trying to plan a trip with my two boys was quite a daunting task with Alan's restaurant schedule and Michael's gallivanting all over the country with his various musical gigs. But we were able to find a few days in June that all three of us had free, almost. A close family friend was getting married on Saturday night, and Michael had to play the organ at the 11:00 church service in Calhoun the next Sunday morning.

I had to be back for a meeting on Thursday so we were wedged into a narrow time slot for this mini-vacation. If we waited on Michael to finish the service and get back to town, it would be after dark before we could get to St. Augustine, and we would basically lose the whole day.

The plan we worked out was for Alan and me to leave early Sunday morning and for my stepson John to pick Michael up after church, drive to the airport in Atlanta where the Georgia Tech Flying Club planes are kept and fly him to the St. Augustine airport. John was a member of the club, and they can reserve and use their planes for just the cost of fuel. He was working on some certification and needed the hours in the air.

It was almost scary how well the plan worked, in spite of the fact that Alan and I missed the exit to Interstate-10 at Lake City in a huge rainstorm while downing our fast food lunch at seventy miles an hour. We realized our mistake after a couple of exits and had to backtrack. We still made it to our destination a little early and had time to hit a small bucket of practice balls at the Royal St. Augustine Golf Club, a golf course that we passed on the way to the airport.

As we walked through the tiny terminal and out the back door, we saw three figures emerge from a small craft on the tarmac. They were some distance away, but two of the shapes looked familiar to us. The airport folks let us walk across to meet them and John introduced us to Guiermo, also a pilot, who had flown down with them to provide John with some company on the return trip to Atlanta.

We said our adieus and headed to our motel on Crescent Beach when we realized we still had enough daylight to get in a round of golf, one of the main reasons for this excursion. After the first nine holes on the narrow course, we all agreed we were either too tired or just playing too badly to finish out the back half. We had lost a bunch of balls between us and decided a good night's rest would reaffirm our game.

As we drove through the historic city past Ripley's Believe It or Not, the old fort Castillo de San Marcos, over the Bridge of Lions, and across Anastasia Island past the aromatic Alligator Farm, my mind drifted back fifty years or so to the first time I ever saw the ocean. It was at St. Augustine when I was around ten years old, and my brother, David, was six.

We lived in the Atco Village then, and I remember barely sleeping the night before the trip. Mama and Daddy got us up at four in the morning, and we all piled into our green 1953 Plymouth with Sister, my aunt, and a lunch basket stuffed with fried chicken, deviled eggs, and bread. We also packed bathing suits, fishing rods, beach towels, and whatever else we thought might come in handy on our first trip to the beach.

Back then it was a thirteen-hour drive down the two-lane Highway 41 that was replaced by the four-lane version in the late fifties and by Interstate 75 in the eighties. Our journey began down Tennessee Street in Cartersville, then wound through Emerson, then Acworth, Kennesaw, Marietta, and Smyrna. All of this before reaching Atlanta, which is now only forty-five minutes away. I can't begin to name all the other towns and hamlets we traveled through in middle and south Georgia, but it was a long, slow trip to say the least.

When Sister didn't travel with us, we had a little more room in the back seat where David and I always played the "Don't Get on My Side" game all the way to where we were going. Many times we were so serious about it that we both earned whippings on the dusty shoulder somewhere en route. This time Sister had to sit between us and served as part barrier and part referee for what seemed to be an eternity.

I remember finally getting to Florida and stopping at a Stuckey's, or some other such operation, which dotted the trek to the Sunshine State. They had slot machines in a back room, and I won twelve dimes on the first pull. I had never seen a one-armed bandit but soon learned where it gets its name. Before we left that wretched place, I had sunk my entire winnings back into the infernal contraption plus half the money I had saved for miniature golf and souvenirs.

We got off of 41 just after lunch and headed east toward the Atlantic Ocean, and it was hot, very hot. We struggled on toward the east coast, with car windows wide open seeking some relief from the stifling Florida heat. Air conditioning did not exist in those days in houses, motels, or cars. We counted cows, played road sign alphabet, and anything else we could think of to pass the time, stopping at red lights and stop signs in every little town we passed through.

Eleven hours into our Florida trip, we finally reached A1A and headed south, searching for a place to spend our two weeks. We passed through St. Augustine and continued south looking for a Vacancy sign. It was somewhere along that stretch that we caught our first glimpse of the mighty Atlantic. It went on forever and my first reaction was that the world looked upside-down, all that blue to the horizon with the sky reflected in its lapping waves. I will never forget the taste of salt on my lips as we drove down the beach road with my head hanging out the window as far as it would go.

In the southern part of St. Augustine Beach, Daddy spotted the subject of our search at a small motel called Sylvan Court. He hung a left and went in to check out the place. We all piled out assuming we had found our new home, and David and I raced across the parking area to try and get a closer glimpse of the ocean that we could hear roaring over the shallow, sea oat-covered sand dunes.

The accommodations were typical of early fifties Florida motels with concrete block walls inside and out, and hard surface, slick terrazzo floors in each room. The steel casement windows were rusted firm at various degrees of openness. The center of the door had crank out jalousie, translucent glass panels, a couple of which were chipped, and one completely missing. It mattered not to us, as we had found our summer haven.

The terrazzo floors had a fine layer of sand that, when swept, immediately re-appeared. We soon learned that this was part of the Florida experience and we just needed to adjust to it. We also learned that this magic ingredient managed to find its way into all the china, silverware, glasses, towels, bed linens, and even into the peanut butter sandwiches.

The parking lot outside consisted of small seashells that were partially ground up, and even the aggregate in the concrete was made up of shells. It all smelled like dead fish. Even in the car when we went sightseeing, which we did in the middle of the day when the sun was too hot to be at the beach, the odor was present. We hit such places as Ripley's Believe It Or Not, the downtown "oldest city" district, the old fort, and the fishing pier.

My personal favorite was the Alligator Farm. Despite the smell, the large reptiles were fascinating, and the snake show presented by Ross Allen, which included the milking of a large diamondback rattlesnake, was spellbinding. A few years later I would stage my own little snake show, but that is another story.

We all had bad dreams for the rest of the trip about the various creatures we witnessed at this classic venue. A monkey exhibit was also featured, and some of their little antics left David and me with questions the folks preferred to dodge.

The fishing pier was also a popular destination for everyone, except David and Sister. Both missed out on the love of fishing Mama and I had inherited from Papa Watkins. We spent hours on the pier for several days and even did some surf fishing on the beach at Sylvan Court where we caught whiting. We didn't know what they were at first, but when schools came by they would jump up completely out of the water. We later learned that they were jumping to elude a larger predator, which added a degree of adventure to our waist-deep angling experience.

From the pier Mama caught a large king mackerel, Daddy nabbed a couple of flounder, and I caught a pompano, which they told us was supposed to be one of the best tasting saltwater fish. The consensus was that the whiting were just as good as the pompano, and we had a lot more of them. I finally managed to snag a sheepshead on a line lowered by hand next to one of the pier pilings using a fiddler crab (a single claw miniature we caught on the inland waterway) for bait. Success came only after employing a technique suggested by an old gentleman on the pier who told me, "Ya gotta jerk des' a'foe deh bite."

In my spare time, of which there was plenty, I scoured the area for the little green lizards that change color when they find themselves on different surfaces. They are not true chameleons, but that's what we called them. I also caught a few of those black lizards with the yellow stripes and blue tails that come off. They were not as sophisticated as the green ones, but it was just as much fun to chase my brother David around the motel parking lot with one of them.

My fondest memory occurred on our trip to the grocery store. Short pants for men were just becoming accepted in the early fifties. Daddy had resisted the trend through most of the trip, but the Florida temperature convinced him to give them a try. He finally gave in and donned a pair of dark brown Bermuda shorts, as they were called then. David, with his knack for naming things, called them "Moo-de-alls".

We finished our shopping and went with Mama to get the car so we could swing by the busy front door of the supermarket and pick Daddy up. As we approached, there he stood with a huge bag of groceries in each hand and about two inches of the legs of his baby blue boxer shorts sticking out below his dark brown shorts and accented against his white legs. It was quite a sight for all to behold.

We were laughing so hard Mama couldn't get stopped and had to circle the entire parking lot before picking him up. He was so angry I thought he was going to kill us all when he got in the car. He didn't. And he also didn't wear shorts for a long, long time after that.

Nine: **Spooks**

When Jane and I got married in 1985, we each brought along a couple of kids ranging in age from six to twelve, three boys and a girl. At first we lived in both sides of a duplex that I bought after my divorce but later moved into what we lovingly refer to as "The Barn." We needed a place big enough for the six of us and, at the time, we didn't have a pot to, uh, cook in, and "The Barn" fulfilled our needs.

It was built in 1887 with solid masonry two story walls, eleven-foot ceilings, a steep pitched roof, and a layer of natural concrete-colored stucco that had been added to cover the cracks in the original brick. It sits on a corner lot with no driveway from Douglas Street, which it faces. Roughly laid brick formed a broken path from the driveway off Carter Street to the back porch, and there was a large piece of marble inlaid in the walk about half way to the house.

The residence once belonged to the county sheriff, who had been murdered in the street beside the back yard, and there were stories about his occasional haunting of the premises. There was even conjecture that he was buried under the marble slab in the walk behind the back porch. We never encountered his apparition, but the place looked the part with the soaring roof and ivy firmly in control of the stucco on the two street sides. It was a perfect place for scaring the heck out of the neighborhood kids on Halloween, and we took full advantage of that for a number of years.

I was working in Dalton when we bought the house, and two days before closing I got a call informing me that termites had basically consumed the front porch. Our options were to put off the purchase or have the porch removed. The loan company required a termite letter vowing that none of these little critters were chomping away at their collateral.

We opted to dismantle the porch since we had already lined up help to move and had someone interested in renting the duplex we were vacating. When we first saw the house without the porch we thought, "What have we done?" A three-foot drop from the front door to the middle of a patch of red clay with a few remnants of the concrete footings scattered about greeted those venturing out of the main entrance.

Not being in the best financial position, we were forced to live in this porch-less abode for over two years. After that length of time we were beginning to get used to it, and it did present us with some decorating options for haunting the ancient place at Halloween. The old porch foundation wall formed an enclosure for our little "graveyard," complete with old column piers serving perfectly as headstones along with some imported concrete blocks. The area was garnished with wilted flowers in green plastic pots, several jack-o-lanterns and a few hay bales and cobwebs included for effect. All-in-all, the place looked pretty darn spooky.

As the trick-or-treaters made their way up the short walkway, they had to step over the old foundation wall and enter the domain of the spirits. They knocked on the bottom stile of the door, and when we opened it their heads only came to about our knees. Even donning a limited costume, I am sure that we made quite an intimidating impression on the dressed up pranksters standing on the ground below.

We were finally able to have the porch rebuilt to the delight of all our neighbors. We continued the annual haunt with varying degrees of effort and success. One year we ended up with a face painting kit someone had given Alan for his birthday. We decided it was time to get serious about our attire and presentation for the trick-or-treaters who would soon be flooding our front porch on this special evening.

Michael rigged up a tape recorder and put a couple of large speakers on the front porch. Just as the kids hit the steps, we would trip the recorder and play some loud, scary organ music.

That got their attention. When they knocked, Alan slowly pulled the squeaky door open from behind to reveal an eight-foot tall figure in white.

We had done an award winning make-up job on my face with the cosmetic kit, and I had a king sized sheet around my head and body that draped to the floor concealing the chair I was standing on. I held a lighted candle near my head that illuminated my ghoulish countenance. Wide-eyed with mouths agape, the kids' focus would slowly climb up my colossal façade. As their stare fell on my blackened eye sockets, I would bend down close to the masked visitors and say, in a screechy whisper, "Yeeessss?"

The brave few that stuck around, mumbled some broken syllables that sounded vaguely like "trick or treat." Just then Alan, bearing the candy bowl, appeared around the door in his black, hooked garb and Marty Feldman grin and let out a high pitched "Tee, hee, hee, hee," in his perfect Igor voice. We had plenty of candy left over that Halloween and noticed for weeks afterward that kids walking to school always crossed the street as they approached our place.

These little plays we put on reminded me of my old snake-catching buddy, Cliff Dyar. Soon after he moved from Rockmart into the Atco village, I learned of a fascinating hobby that he had pursued for many years ... makeup. I don't mean the girlie type, but materials used by real moviemakers of our day to transform normal people into a variety of creatures from the Black Lagoon to the castles of Transylvania.

Today, computer animation has taken over a large part of the task of creating theatrical monsters, but in the early days, geniuses like Lon Chaney worked magic with this craft. Cliff idolized Chaney for the magic he could work with disguises. He studied books written by Chaney and others on how to create realistic wounds and afflictions. Cliff also had an extensive repertory of heinous monster faces he could call up in a matter of minutes. His secret was a professional makeup kit he owned that bore the name of his champion.

Often Cliff would get out his bag of tricks and cook up a face that even a mother, his mother, couldn't look at, let alone love. And she was a registered nurse accustomed to seeing some pretty terrible things. More than once she threatened to flush his sinister makings down the toilet.

One special day each year, the last day of October, presented us with an opportunity to showcase Cliff's talent. Now this particular evening takes on a whole different character in a mill village. It is difficult to say who spends the evening in greater peril, the haunters or the hauntees. As younger kids, we watched the day approach with mixed expectations of great delight and pure horror. There was no age limit for the participants and between the older kids intent on relieving you of your treats, being egged, and the residents who greeted you with a loaded shotgun, the night offered plenty of excitement.

One favorite trick among the older guys was to get a brown paper bag and fill it with, well uh, waste, I guess is a polite way to say it. This sack of, ahem, stuff, was placed on the porch of some unpopular resident. Then a match set the top of the sack ablaze. The trickster would then pound on the door and run to a hidden vantage point to watch the object of this foul trick stamp out the fire on his wooden porch. Anyone within two blocks had their vocabulary expanded as the victim discovered what was in the bag and was now all over his shoes.

This is not the kind of thing that Cliff and I did. We took the high road and just tried to scare the hell out of some of the younger kids as they traversed a shortcut through the park in front of the mill. It was very dark there and a perfect place for a real monster to jump out and grab you.

We were not the type to take a treat bag by force but were not opposed to picking one up that might slip from the fingers of a fleeing eight-year-old screaming his lungs out.

We repeated this Halloween ambush caper for several years at differing locations around the park to keep big brothers from catching on and spoiling our fun ... and our makeup. I don't think anyone ever figured out who the real monsters were, and it was awfully hard not to give it away when it came up in the harrowing stories the kids passed around the village.

The last year we did our little show we decided to spice it up with a little dramatic action. When a group of our young neighbors would approach one of the big magnolia trees near the center of the park, I would ease onto the path ahead of them. I walked toward them until I was about ten feet away. Cliff would then jump out from behind the tree and grab me. He was dressed like Dracula, and his face was made up to resemble anything but a human. He would make all sorts of growling noises, and I would scream and struggle as he dragged me off into the bushes on the other side of the path.

Six pairs of wide eyes, illuminated by the full moon, stood frozen for a moment. When the scene they had just witnessed registered in their gray matter, they pushed their motor skills to the limit and disappeared in an instant. We would share a good laugh then move on to another path to repeat our little antic.

Setting up for our fourth location, we heard voices in the distance approaching our staging area. They were deep voices, and didn't sound very friendly, with muffled words like "teach them a lesson" punctuated with a variety of very descriptive adjectives and family references describing their target, which apparently was us.

We could make out the silhouettes of five large bodies heading in our direction from the front side of the park. To our rear and side was the fence that separated the mill from the rest of the village. We were trapped with nothing for protection but Cliff's ugly, made-up face.

We took shelter under a nearby magnolia, fighting through the leaves and low branches to a spot near the trunk. Now the magnolia trees in the park were left to grow as nature intended and the lower tier of boughs drug the ground. We hoped this would help keep us hidden from the nearing interlopers with designs on modifying our current state of health.

It was dark, very dark. Luckily we both had on black clothing for our little performance, so the main thing we had to hide was our skin anywhere it showed, and Cliff's fake, white, glowing countenance. We buried our faces in the heavy layer of fallen, decomposing foliage with our arms over our heads. The dry leaf bed below our bodies loudly protested our presence, and we had to remain perfectly still to assure our sanctuary.

We could hear the vigilantes parting the heavy, magnolia branches speaking in angry voices all at the same time. Then a strange, crackling sound began to fill the air mixed with excited utterances from our pursuers. As the tempo and clamor of the hullabaloo expanded, I tilted my head slightly to catch a glimpse of what had transpired. These geniuses had used matches to try and spot us and one had fallen into the ground cover, setting it ablaze. They were all stomping and slapping at the growing flames under the tree, an action that only seemed to promote the fire's intensity.

I am sure we were in plain sight by then, but the distraction allowed us time to sneak out the other side of the magnolia and head for home. As we made it to the edge of the park we met Mr. Padgett, the night shift policeman in full stride, flashlight in hand, and we knew these guys were in real trouble. It was the fastest we had seen an Atco policeman run since the afternoon of the Nancy Creek invasion, but that is another story.

As we sat on the front porch, still breathing hard from our little adventure, we agreed this would be the last year for our Halloween exhibition. This had been too close a call, risking life and limb, for a simple night of haunting the park.

Ten: **Street Show**

In the middle of a rather frantic afternoon at the office, I was interrupted by a visit from Charles, the person who keeps our yard looking glorious in spite of the heavy tree cover and a three-year drought. He and his crew also tend to my mother's yard, and he had come to collect for his recent work there.

After writing his check and telling him what a wonderful job he was doing, I asked him to schedule another task at her house when his crew could get to it. My mother had been after me for months to mention it to Charles, but I had not remembered it until now.

My Dad, before he passed away five years earlier, had a large vegetable garden plot that he nourished for about forty years. It was somewhat famous around town, and his tomatoes were so sweet he had been accused of using sugar in place of fertilizer by some of the recipients of his harvests. It was certainly the most fertile spot of ground in town, if not in all of North Georgia.

Unfortunately, Daddy did not pass down his green thumb or any hint of a desire to plant, fertilize, till, weed, and all those other things you have to do in the red clay to be a success at gardening. The only thing I have been able to grow was a full beard back in the seventies, and my younger brother is having enough trouble keeping his hair from wilting.

If you have ever had a garden of any size, from two plants to twenty rows, you undoubtedly have experienced the growth rate of weeds and other foreign botanical marvels that appear without invitation seemingly overnight. In two days they can dwarf your precious petunias, snap dragons, and daffodils and overpower your potatoes, tomatoes, and butter peas. Only hours on hands and knees or bending over a hoe can stave off these wonders of natural selection.

Well, that's what they can do even when you are dedicated to the daily battle with these sprouts. When you let them go for a week or so, it becomes difficult to find your plants, and after a month you can hardly recognize it as a garden. After five years, well, need I say, the weeds had gone completely wild. There were even several trees that stood well over ten feet high.

You now have a sense of the daunting challenge I was asking Charles to undertake. During our discussion we decided it would be best if he waited until winter when his lawn mowing demands were less stringent. I also happened to mention that it would also be a good time since snakes would be hibernating.

"Snakes!" I could see Charles begin to squirm in his chair at the thought, and I could not resist relating one of my snake stories to him. It happened while we still lived in the Atco Mill Village one hot summer afternoon.

I had been collecting snakes for several years and had three cages of differing sizes where I kept my "pets." I had something of a reputation for my reptilian interest around the village. If nothing else, it kept me safe, as a skinny twelve-year-old, from the normal bullying and threats to which some of my peers were subjected. I can still hear the warnings conveyed to a potential antagonist, "He'll put a snake on you if you mess with him."

The favorite, and almost constant, summer pastime in the village was the swimming pool, a beautiful, white ceramic tile structure. It was drained and refilled each week with well water and was crystal clear, although a bit chilly.

Every morning after breakfast, we would put on our bathing suits and walk, or run if the pavement was hot, to the pool two blocks away from our back door. At noon we rushed home for a quick dinner that we ate in wet bathing suits. Back then we didn't have lunch, just dinner and supper. As soon as we finished, we returned to the pool and stayed until they ran us out. We would all get sunburned a couple of times in early June, but eventually it turned to a tan that seemed to protect our young and tender bodies for the remainder of the summer.

One afternoon I was walking home at about the time of the four o'clock shift change and noticed a large crowd of several hundred people gathered around in the middle of the street in front of our house. We lived on Goodyear Avenue, the main street leading into the village from Cassville Road, and almost everybody walked past our place on the way to and from the mill. On this day it seemed that everybody from both the first and second shifts was standing in the road.

Approaching the throng through a narrow opening in the three-foot high, neatly trimmed privet hedge that bordered all the yards in the village, I heard several whispers of, "There he is," and, "Here he comes," emanate from the group. As I neared the circle, barefoot, wearing only my bathing suit, the mass of humanity began to part like the Red Sea.

The focus of the large gathering became obvious as I made my way through the opening the crowd created upon my approach. There in the center, coiled for business, was the six-foot long, gray rat snake that had escaped from my cage three days earlier. This large specimen was a gift from Mr. Sutton, one of the security policemen who occupied the small building we called the policeman's shack at the corner of our yard across from the mill. He had a farm out in the county and occasionally brought me a snake that he had captured.

This was one of the biggest I had ever had in my collection, and his black and gray-splotched body was thicker than my arm. Even when I held his head as high as I could reach, this snake's tail still drug the ground. During my stay in the Atco Village Mr. Sutton brought me some very interesting specimens, but this was the largest and most intimidating of the lot.

My old reptilian friend was obviously agitated by all the attention he was receiving, and he hissed and lunged at the multitude that surrounded him. The crowd had left plenty of space between the front row and the object of their gathering, which presented me with quite a unique stage to perform my "death defying" act.

A hush fell over the crowd as I entered the arena. I paused for a moment to take stock of the situation and determine the safest way to corral the rat snake with the limited accessories at my immediate disposal. I decided to chance it and address the situation head on with bare hands and feet, giving my audience something to talk about in the process.

Slowly and deliberately I raised my hands, pointing in the general direction of the reptile as I took a step forward. This motion received an audible "ooooh" from the mob. I knew that I had tamed the constrictor over the duration of his captivity, but with all the excitement, he was obviously very unhappy. I had to exercise extreme caution because, even though my friend was not poisonous, a specimen this size could inflict a very nasty and painful bite.

As I eased forward, the crowd shifted slightly to the rear with a slow inhalation that could be sensed if not actually heard. I made a large, sweeping circle around the huge snake with my hands still raised. His head followed my every step, with eyes fixed upon mine and his forked tongue rapidly flicking out in my direction. I paused for a moment and slowly, very slowly, reached out toward the writhing form with my right hand as the workers held their collective breath.

As the recoiled head tensed, the serpent's tail began to vibrate against some dry leaves on the rough asphalt paving producing an audible buzzing sound. This is a normal reaction for most snake species, but the rattlesnake is the only one with the equipment to sound his ominous warning.

As anxious whispers of "rattler" echoed through the crowd, the cornered animal suddenly lunged at my outstretched hand. Only my quick reflexes prevented the behemoth from scoring a direct hit. With this strike, the entire front row jumped back a step producing a domino effect that rippled through to the rear of the pack resulting in numerous stepped-on toes and a few near falls. The whole bunch let out a yelp that could be heard over the entire village.

I could barely keep from laughing, and it took all my concentration to keep a straight face and to continue to make the situation look as perilous as I could. At this point I knew I had their undivided attention, and it was definitely "Showtime."

I eased in a little closer and circled the hissing reptile again with my bare feet only inches out of striking range. I could hear the excited whispers being exchanged by my audience from all directions as I continued my patient stalking. I never spoke a word, just concentrated my gaze on the animal that followed me with its coiled body slowly, around and around.

Then another strike, this time at my ankle, and another quick jerk kept my tender flesh out of harms way. The crowd's reaction repeated, tapering only slightly from the first, and continued with each attempt of the serpent to connect with my near naked body. I was sweating by now, and the droplets forming on my upper body glistened in the afternoon sun adding a further sense of urgency to the proceedings.

After ten or fifteen minutes and some calming hand motions and soft utterances to my old friend, I was able to gently pick him up and raise his body slowly as he coiled around my hands and arms. This was the coup-de-grâce. Every eye was as wide open as a kid's on Christmas morning, and it seemed as though everybody was talking and pointing at once. As I began moving toward my house, a huge opening appeared in seconds allowing for my uninterrupted departure.

I walked across the sidewalk, through the hedges, and around my side yard to the cages behind the house. I departed without a word or a backward glance.

I uncoiled the gray rat snake from my arms, returned him to his temporary home, and locked the cage door. Several loose nails holding the wire to the wood frame had allowed him to escape. They were again secured. I changed the water in his dish then sat down and talked with him for a while about how happy it made me to have him back home, assuring him he would be safe as long as he didn't run away again.

A couple of hours later, I happened to glance out the front window of the living room and noticed a large crowd, about half the size of the original, still milling around in the street, talking and occasionally pointing over toward our front porch.

My reputation had been reconfirmed as a fearless snake handler, and I was assured of future protection from those who might want to cause me harm, all by the simple threat of the living biological weapons at my disposal.

Eleven: **The Trails**

The Saturday morning air was on the chilly side under an overcast sky as we backed the truck from receptacle to receptacle tossing our load of various junk into the bins at the Burnt Hickory Road recycling center. Jane and I had finally gotten up the nerve to tackle what was the old dirt-floored coal bin of our ancient house that had become the graveyard for a variety of implements and furnishings that had outlived their usefulness.

The space was intended to be used as a storeroom for garden and other outdoor tools but had, over the past ten years, become so packed with refuse that we barely had access to the gear that belonged there. An old plastic Christmas tree stand that leaked, the frame of a lawn chair with no webbing, rusted paint cans, scraps of wood, a wheelbarrow with a broken handle, along with other such stuff filled up the back of our red Toyota pickup.

As I peered into the last of the large waste containers to deposit the final item, a corroded grill, the contents I observed reminded me of another such place of refuse that we had out at Atco. It was the garbage dump on top of a hill on the backside of the village that we called trash hill.

All kinds of interesting things could be found there if one felt the urge to do a little exploring and excavating. The piles of rubbish and various other cast-away articles shifted around a bit between excursions, and there always seemed to be a small fire smoldering somewhere in the heaps.

We were not supposed to hang around trash hill, or trash pile hill as some called it, where the air always smelled of sweet and sour rubbish punctuated by the acrid odor similar to that of a house fire a block away. Many times we would sneak off to the hill with our BB guns to shoot at rats. Some of them were so big they would just sit there and laugh at you in the rare event that your aim was on target. It was said that cats in the village were afraid to prowl around trash hill.

Just to the left of the dump lay two dirt paths that led down a steep hill to Pettit Creek. These routes terminated at a pair of cable crossings that offered alternative routes over the creek and into town for those who lived on the south side of Atco known as the "New Village."

These wire bridges presented a great opportunity for us kids when things got a bit boring on the streets or at the playground. They were considered off limits by parents because they crossed the water at two of the narrowest and deepest points of the creek. Obviously, this made them irresistibly attractive to a bunch of twelve-year-olds in search of excitement brought on by flirting with certain danger.

Each of the crossing locations featured a steel post about eight feet high with a half inch wide metal cable fastened near the top and another several inches off the ground. These strands ran across the water to a similar support on the other bank. They were spaced so that you could stand on the lower cable and reach up and grab the upper wire with your hands. By sliding alternate hands and feet you could make your way across the barrier in relative safety; that is, unless someone on the bank decided to shake the cable.

This distraction occurred quite frequently and led to pleas and threats from the one midway across the water and sometimes resulted in a fully clothed dunking. This risk was especially high at the cable furthest away from Cassville Road.

The nearer crossing had very taught lines making the passage somewhat easier, even when being manipulated by antagonists on the bank. The other wire bridge, however, had a great deal of slack in the upper line causing your body to sway back and forth increasing the difficulty factor significantly. We soon learned not to test our prowess at this crossing.

The two routes that led down to the cables were part of a network of paths that ran up and down and across a steep, sixty-foot drop in a wooded area that we called the trails. This was the closest thing we had to an off-road bike track, and we spent many hours there showing off our cycling abilities and bravado.

A trail along the top of the ridge started at trash hill and terminated at the top of the last downward route. It was the steepest of the four trails and was interrupted by flat spots where two lateral paths crossed it. These level areas made perfect launching ramps for daring souls willing to risk life and limb sailing through the air at a very high rate of speed between the tree trunks that loomed on each side.

I never quite got up the nerve to try that particular ride, but my best friend and next-door-neighbor, Boyce, could not walk away from a dare. Someone, not me of course, laid down the "double dog" on him and to the top of the hill he headed. He had to push his bike because the trail was so steep no one could climb it in the saddle. All we had in those days were the heavy, one-speed, what you peddle is what you get, twenty-inch bicycles.

After a long pause at the crest of the rise, his eyes began to focus through those glasses that he had worn since birth, and his chest expanded with a long, deep breath. He stood up on the pedals and began his date with destiny down the steepest path "the trails" had to offer.

Now you must understand that this particular vertical slope had a reputation in the village, and the story was that only one person had ever successfully negotiated its full length. Most chickened out shortly after the initial pedal release and hit their brakes, laying the bike down before ever reaching the first jump.

Those who dared to stay in the saddle past the first path usually struck the ground at an angle that flipped them sideways to the dirt. From there a series of circles carried them toward the bottom of the hill until they met up with one or more of the many trees that crowded the route. Those daredevils received many a bump and bruise, and even a few broken bones, but by some stroke of luck and by the grace of God, no one had received a serious injury.

Word of such challenges spread fast in the village. By the time Boyce was ready to begin his descent, a large crowd had gathered and was mingling among the thick stand of trees awaiting the main event. All had heard the tales about past endeavors on the treacherous venue, and a wave of excitement rippled through the group in anticipation of this attempt.

With all eyes glued on his tense form, Boyce released the brake and leaned forward over the front wheel as he began his run. He rapidly gained speed but was able to maintain control for the top portion of the trek. When he reached the first horizontal intersection, his body rose off the seat as his vehicle went airborne. He hung on to the handlebars through the short flight, and it appeared he might be able to recover.

His wheels touched down just before the second cross path, and his fanny hit the seat just as the craft encountered the next jump in his wild ride. It wasn't pretty. The combination of the bike coming up to meet Boyce's downward moving body produced a thud that almost muffled the cry of pain issued by the rider. The next thing I knew, his limp form was making a large loop over the handlebars. It all played out in slow motion as he made contact with the ground, his trusty bike in hot pursuit.

At this point I, along with the rest of the gathered mass, realized it was time to do what all smart village kids do in this situation: run like hell. Whether it be a loud noise, like an adult shouting, a kid screaming, a whistle blaring, a siren wailing, or some sort of accident, we all knew instinctively to get as far away as we could as soon as possible.

When I topped the hill heading to the village, I glanced back and saw what appeared to be a fistfight between my good friend and his trusty red bicycle spinning in the midst of a moving cloud of dust nearing the bottom of the incline. I jumped on my own bike and peddled down Mayflower Street toward home as fast as my little legs would carry me. I had this sinking feeling that I may never see my good buddy again.

I was very relieved when Boyce showed up at my door the next morning ready to take on another day of adventure courtesy of the village. He was a bit sore and a little skinned up, but no mention was made of the previous day's near death experience. He did say he would like to play some games around the yard for a day or two while his bicycle was being repaired at the shop.

The two of us were about as close to brothers as kids could be. We had lived next door to each other since we were four years old and were almost always together, playing outside or at one of our houses. School was an exception where his "T" placed him in Mrs. Brandon's first grade class and my "H" sent me to Miss Amy's. This alphabetical arrangement kept us from ever being in the same class.

His mother, Irma, was a nurse and helped us all stay in one piece in spite of the efforts we put into various forms of self-destruction. She was a no-nonsense, Ohio native, and she knew how to get our attention in matters of discipline, with her high-pitched voice and "Yankee" accent.

I felt like I was loosing my right arm when I heard that Boyce's dad, Ray, had accepted a position with the Goodyear Plant in Decatur, Alabama, and he would be moving at the end of our sixth grade year at Cherokee Avenue School. I had never had to deal with such a loss at my young age, and it literally took me years to get over it.

We did visit back and forth after he moved. I loved going over to Decatur in the summers and riding on the back of Boyce's Harley Davidson. At that time in Alabama you could get a license to drive a motorcycle at fourteen, and Boyce and a bunch of his buddies ran paper routes on their Harleys to pay for them. I tried my hand at the newspaper delivery business back at home, but that is another story.

We kept in communication during our high school days, and when it came time to make a college decision, Boyce chose Georgia Tech where his older brother Robert was enrolled. He knew I planned to go there too, and contacted me about being roommates. We made the necessary application arrangements and received notification that we would be paired in Brown Dorm, the oldest one Tech had to offer. But we didn't care; we were going off to our favorite college, together.

Twelve: **Cool Cool Water**

It was high tide late in the afternoon as Michael and I fought the surf to get out to the breakers off Crescent Beach, which is just south of St. Augustine. The waves were breaking at a point about belly deep, and they were so big and coming so fast that it made the trek difficult. At low tide these same swells broke in shallower water making it much easier to reach the spot that offered the best raft surfing. The waves were particularly large this day due to a tropical depression just off the coast.

To avoid the most dangerous rays, we generally waited until the sun was low over the land behind us before venturing into the foamy broth. Unfortunately, low tide happened closer to noon on this particular trip, so we had to take what we could get, which put the surf action out further than we preferred.

Alan was at our place in Beacher's Lodge watching us from the balcony with binoculars. He had seen the movie "Jaws" one time too many and wanted little to do with the waves that challenged us more adventurous ones. As it happened, we only had two rafts, so the situation worked pretty well.

As we paused between breakers, I related to Michael the story of a Florida trip the family took when I was about his age. We were staying at Sylvan Court, near our present location, when a similar storm was again in the area. His granddaddy and I had a very similar experience with huge waves that you could ride all the way in until your knees dragged on the sand in the shallow water. This old, classic, concrete block "Mom and Pop" motel had given way years earlier to condominiums and high-rise apartments that now dot the once pristine beach areas.

On our way back to the room as the sun disappeared behind our building and the sea breeze began to wane, we decided to stop off for a brief dip in the pool. It was tucked in the courtyard of our temporary quarters and reflected the colors presented by the fading sun on the puffy clouds above.

Before entering, we showered to rid our bodies of the beach sand and salt residue that clung to us and made our way to the pool steps. Anticipating the cool chilling waters, I stuck my right foot into the lapping surface. It was hot, not just warm, but hot. At least that's what it seemed to me at the time. I guess it had soaked up all the energy the Florida sun threw at it during the almost cloudless day.

We jumped in, even though the air above felt cooler on our bodies than the bluish clear, chlorine-scented basin. I swam a couple of laps and did a few surface dives, but it somehow didn't offer the refreshing chill I had anticipated.

In stark contrast, I thought of the pool in the Atco Village where I grew up. Now that was a cold-water pool, and I do mean cold. It was not the circulating, filtered arrangement that is most common today. It was completely drained every Wednesday afternoon and scrubbed down by the crew of lifeguards, then refilled overnight with well water, fifty-five degrees at best. It opened about mid-morning Thursday, and in less than twenty minutes even the most conditioned patron started to turn blue. One big toe was about as much as any of my visiting friends from town, accustomed to the city pool, were able to submerge.

During the summer in the village, the pool was our main source of entertainment. We basically spent the entire season in our bathing suits and most of that time in the water. The other big attraction was roller-skating in the evening after the pool closed, but that is another story.

The first challenge upon entering the village swimming area was the dreaded shower, mandatory before we were allowed in its crystal waters. The locker rooms containing the torturous spray were located in the basement of the adjacent school and accessed by a pair of narrow, concrete steps that disappeared below the massive brick building.

The boy's side was always damp and cold and usually smelled like a combination of sweat, stinky feet, pee, and a wet dog. It was dimly illuminated by under-wattage, incandescent bulbs, which were suspended on long power cords from the raw concrete ceiling.

As if the shower did not present adequate intimidation, all prospective swimmers had to wade through a thin pan placed in front of the two shower stalls filled with milky-colored, ice-cold water that smelled like lye soap with a hint of chlorine. These shallow vessels were six feet square, and there was no physical way to avoid splashing through them.

Once past the toe-tingling brew, you found yourself in a tiny, concrete cubicle with a floor that sloped to a small drain. A half-inch pipe with a thin chain attached to a spring-loaded valve handle ran up the wall to a rusty showerhead. When pulled, a gush of cold water filled the space and doused your body with well water. Yes, the same well water that filled the pool, except fresher and colder.

There was no hot water at all and no way to adjust the volume of the cold. It was on full blast or off completely. You learned quickly to protect your vulnerable body parts from the torrent or pay the painful consequences.

Once cleansed, you ventured through the milky water again and were then qualified to enter the hallowed realm of the lifeguards. This feared group of semi-adults wielded supreme rule over the confines of the pool area, and they would kick anyone out for the least infraction. Running, pushing, not taking a proper shower, or just looking at them wrong could get you a holiday from the fun and frolic.

J. V. Simpson was one of these entrusted individuals. He always wore dark glasses with a string attached to keep them from falling into the pool when he got excited, which was often. He sat in the eight-foot-high lifeguard stand adjacent to the gate leading to the showers. This position provided an excellent vantage point to nab those who failed to properly prepare for entry. A silver whistle, suspended by a colorful woven lanyard, dangled from his neck. The shrill report issued by this tiny instrument was the signal to freeze in your tracks and direct your attention to the trumpeter. Someone was headed home.

The only other lifeguard I remember was named Weaver. I can't recall his first name but most people called him "Bugle Butt." I didn't know what that meant for a long time, but when someone told me, it fit the bill.

He always wore a light tan "Jungle Jim" hat and shades that were so dark you couldn't see through them. He took them off one time near the end of summer exposing a stark white circle around each eye. It was really very spooky looking.

There were actually two separate pools in the village. The "big" pool had an eight-foot deep end below a ten-foot diving board, and it sloped up to the shallow end that measured about three feet. The pool was white ceramic tile, made up of one-inch squares with green tiled stripes on the bottom defining six racing lanes that ran lengthwise.

Green tiled numerals down the sides of the pool marked the distance in five-foot increments from five at the deep end to seventy at the shallow end. A green stripe around the perimeter marked the water level, and a heavy rope threaded through a series of large steel rings surrounded the swimming area to assist in exiting the frigid waters.

The baby pool was adjacent to the shallow end of the big pool and was separated by a tiled wall a foot thick with a steel pipe rail on top. A sliding board spanned the smaller pool at its midpoint. The steps were on one side and led up to the slide that started about twelve feet high over the center of the baby pool and extended ten feet into the shallow end of the big pool. Cold water was piped to the top of the slide and sprayed down the surface to hasten the descent into the big pool.

Most of us little guys just sat on our butts or went head first on our bellies, but the older boys played another game. They would stand on the third and sometimes fourth step from the top and grab the two side handles that went up about two feet above the top of the ladder. They then jumped as high as they could and flung themselves up and over the top of the ladder landing on their knees on the sliding surface well down toward the water. The game was to see how far they could fly before landing on the slide and then how far out into the pool they could dive.

This was obviously a rather dangerous use of the sliding board, and the lifeguard tossed out many a swimmer for engaging in this activity. It continued nonetheless, until the day one of the more gutsy souls lost his heading in mid-jump and straddled the ridge on one side of the slide on his way to a headlong plunge into the foot-deep baby pool below. He did manage to walk away from the incident, but he was in obvious pain.

Big kids were not allowed in the baby pool and one evening, a young rookie lifeguard was having trouble enforcing the rule. As soon as he chased a big kid out, another jumped in from the other end. An older gentleman who was seated on a bench outside the fence was watching the antics of the older boys. He called one over and said something to him. The boy spread the message and immediately all the big guys vacated the scene.

The wise old man had simply asked the menacing kid if he knew why the water was always warmer in the baby pool.

At the opposite end of the pool stood the three-meter diving board. We didn't know what a meter was back then. We just knew it as "the board" that was ten feet high. We had no lower diving board, as do most pools, so we had to go off the high dive or be relegated to diving off the pool curb.

I was never brave enough to dive, but my cannonball from the big board was pretty good. This was accomplished by folding feet under fanny and wrapping arms around knees to make a big splash as a large area of the body hit the water at the same time. When done properly, even a small frame could deliver quite a volume of water in the direction opposite the point of entry. When delivered by the hefty body of the two-ton-tank, otherwise known as Hugh Shelby, the resulting geyser was quite a spectacle.

There was a row of steel benches just outside the fence on the opposite side of the pool from the old school. When the pool was open in the evening, sometimes people would gather on the seats to watch the action inside the fence. This presented a tempting target for the cannonball brigade. We would climb the ladder to the board and run off the end in rapid succession and "cannonball" the crowd.

Hugh, the two-ton-tank, was the last in line one evening. After my attempt, I turned just in time to see the sturdy board bend to its limit under his powerful spring that lifted him high in the air. I held my breath as his huge body came perilously close to the pool's edge. Tucking at just the right moment and landing at just the right spot produced a cascade of frigid liquid that totally drenched the fully clothed occupants of the four nearest benches and severely dampened many others.

The crowd's reaction reminded me of what happened when a wasp nest was jabbed with a cane pole. Bodies scattered in all directions for a moment only to return with stinging remarks and profane expressions directed at the "two-ton-tank." He leaped from the pool with great pride and struck a Tarzan-like pose, with hands on hips, as he faced the angry, cursing crowd from within the safety of the six-foot fence.

Suddenly, their furious shouts turned to exuberant laughter as they realized the "Tank" had completely busted the bottom out of his bathing trunks. There he was, standing with the thin, translucent, white mesh that was once the suit liner, draped over his budding manhood. The remainder of his shredded garment was strung down along his left leg well past the knee.

In his moment of glory, he was completely oblivious to the reason for the throng's reaction. Eventually, he glanced downward and realized his situation. He immediately struck the "fig leaf" pose and half dove, half fell into the refuge of the frigid waters and swam to the opposite corner of the pool, completely under water. He quietly surfaced with a raised hand, begging for a towel to provide him with temporary coverage as he escaped to the dressing room.

Thirteen: **Wild Blue Yonder**

The front walk was still damp from an evening shower, and the still air held a heavy, humid sweetness in its grasp as I made my way barefoot to get the Saturday morning paper. The early April rain softened the hard, red, Georgia clay around our mailbox where an errant driver had jumped the curb sometime during the night leaving a very distinct tire print that nearly sideswiped the receptacle.

Jane was still in bed enjoying her first day of Spring Break, and I dared not awaken her. This was the first time in several years she had worked as a full-time school counselor, and she was completely worn out, and ready for this mini-vacation.

Paper in hand, I started back to the house when I noticed numerous green shapes littering the concrete walk and steps. Whirlybirds! Those little green seedlets from the silver maple tree in our front yard literally covered the ground below me.

Instinctively, I picked up the one nearest my bare left foot and tossed it into the early morning air. It fell a short distance then began to twirl rapidly as it made its winding way to a gentle landing. I picked up another and released it higher in the cool air, and it repeated the slow, circular descent to the ground. The zigzag pattern of the petal's flight stirred memories of the Atco Mill Village and the many hours we spent with these hovering gifts from Mother Nature.

Our house in the village was the first one on Goodyear Avenue after you passed between the store and the mill. We were on the same side of the street as the store and diagonally across from the mill. A small, hexagonal wooden structure that housed the village security sat on the corner across Clearwater Street from the store. We called it the "policeman's shack." It had double hung windows on five sides and a door that faced the mill across the intersection.

There were two parking spaces marked off at the corner, one for the patrolman's car and a second for a taxicab that was driven by Mr. Cagle. He only had one leg and got around on crutches. We took his cab to town one time, and I still remember how fascinated I was with the mechanism he had rigged up to allow him to operate a straight shift which was all that was available on his 1940-something Ford.

The corner of our oversized yard started at the policeman's shack and ran along Clearwater in front of the store entrance. For some reason this space, which was big enough for two more houses, had been left open. It made a great play yard for kick-the-can, football, and anything else we could think of and was a magnet for neighborhood kids.

Half way down the street toward the store was a big maple tree. In the spring it released the largest seedlets you could ever imagine. When a gust of leftover March wind stirred its branches, they would unleash the twirling, winged pods that filled the air all around you.

These delightful free toys were placed in service for the duration of their existence and presented a plethora of opportunities for the creative mind. We concocted many different contests using these mini-helicopters.

The highest toss always created a great deal of controversy as each contestant had his eye on his own entry. With as many as eight to ten players, the arguments continued, so we tried appointing judges. The idea seemed valid; but, in reality, a single person could not watch all the twirlers, and many accusations of favoritism were levied.

The slowest decent or last to hit the ground was a little easier to evaluate, but grumbling persisted. If you selected the right shaped pod to begin with, you were the odds-on favorite until someone could locate a finer specimen.

A much easier contest to judge was the accuracy shoot. Using an old twenty-inch bicycle tire as the downwind target, each participant would hurl his selected seed into the breeze trying to land the twirling craft in the defined circle.. The successful ones retrieved their favorite pod and competed in a toss-off, gradually eliminating those who didn't score.

We spent a lot of time looking up during these various contests, and I guess, in a way, it trained us for the next challenge of early fifties life, "The Cold War." During that time growing fears of aggression from Communist powers pervaded the airwaves and the governing entities around the country.

In Atco, they started something called Ground Observation Corps that was a part of the Civil Defense network. Its center of operations was the policeman's shack at the corner of our yard and its primary purpose was to identify and document the time, direction, altitude, and craft type of all planes that flew over or in sight of Atco airspace.

I would go over and "help" them when I had nothing better to do and soon became one of their best spotters with my young pair of eyes. They had little printed cards with pictures of various types of planes that were used to identify and catalogue the sightings. I loved the challenge and have always held a certain fascination with things in the sky.

One clear warm afternoon, my neighbor Boyce and I were spread out on a blanket between our two houses. We were just lying there looking up into the deep blue, cloudless sky talking about whatever twelve-year-olds talk about, when we heard the sound of a jet. Now back then, that was a real rarity, and it caught our attention immediately.

We strained our eyes searching intently in the direction of the distant roar but were unable to locate the source of the noise. As we continued to stare, suddenly, what appeared to be tiny, silver specks began to come into view. They were so faint that I was not even sure they were real until I mentioned it to Boyce, and he said he was seeing them too.

I ran in the house and grabbed Daddy's German binoculars he had brought home from the War. By the time I got back to the blanket, the specks had turned to more of a whitish color, and there were hundreds of them. The view through the powerful binoculars yielded no clue as to the identity of these strange, airborne particles.

As they got closer to the ground, their shape became more linear, and their color had changed to a light, brownish green. They also exhibited a fluttering motion that became more apparent the lower they descended.

We started to follow one that was drifting overhead nearest to us as we watched another disappear over a house a block away. They had become very spread out by this time and the only form we could still see was the one we were chasing. It was still a few hundred feet high as we tracked it up the back alley and across Mayflower Street.

It was headed toward the field behind the Atco Baptist Church a block away, and that is where we were finally able to corral it. What a disappointment. It was, or at least it looked like, a giant leaf from a corn plant, about three and a half feet long and very brittle to the touch. As we passed it back and forth in silence, our gaze alternated between the mysterious object and each other's questioning stare.

We took it home and showed it to Boyce's dad, Ray, and to my dad, and neither had an explanation as to its origin or how it made it to our neighborhood. Several others in the village had also captured one of the alien corn leaves, and it remained a topic of conversation for quite a while.

To this day, I still do not have a clue as to the source of the roar we heard or the arrival of these eerie leaves. The best we have been able to surmise is that some sort of a storm, perhaps a tornado, picked up the foliage from a field in the Midwest, or somewhere, and managed to carry it up into the jet stream where it was transported to the village.

The sky over Atco was dotted with kites from March through May. We could buy a rolled-up kit at the store for a quarter that had all the makings for this flying toy except for the tail and the cord. There were a few box kites available back then, but most of the kites were the standard, oblong rectangle, shaped like a baseball diamond where home plate had been stretched forward into the bleachers.

There was a string around the perimeter of the paper that was exposed at the corners. The two, different-length, struts with slits in both ends could be shaped in place after a little bending and coaxing. When the string was implanted in the grooves, the wrinkles stretched out of the paper skin as the bowed sticks exerted just the right amount of tension.

Once assembled, the four corners of the taut frame were attached to pieces of the string forming a harness of sorts to which the cord roll was tied. What they did not tell you about the kite cord roll was that there was no connection between the end of the line and the cardboard cylinder that held it. Many a kite was lost when the roll came to an end, and the string trailed out across the yard, the house, trees, etc., never to be seen again.

The smart thing to do was to find a spindle from the mill, or a short section of broom handle and tie the end of the kite string to it, then wrap the cord from the wide cardboard cylinder onto the new keeper. This took a while to do, but it was well worth it when the line ran out.

Daddy was the plant engineer at Goodyear, and, with that background, he always wanted to do things a little bigger and a little better than the everyday. One gusty Friday afternoon he decided to build a super-kite. He used thin, very strong lattice strips for the frame and stout twine he brought home from the mill that was used to reinforce tires. It was very thin and almost impossible to break. The final product stood over six feet tall and some four feet wide.

He tied the two ends of the short stick together with the unbreakable twine using just the right amount of tension to create the desired bow in the brown wrapping paper skin. A retired bed sheet, ripped into a three-inch wide streamer, formed the basic tail, which sported short pieces of the discarded linen tied at intervals of about a foot. It was a masterful creation.

The next day we positioned ourselves for the launch in our oversized yard. A small crowd began to gather, as was customary for such events in the village. Daddy handed me the spool with the super-cord wrapped around it, and I fed out about fifty feet while he walked downwind doing his best to steady the craft in the strong west wind. The paper skin rattled in anticipation, and the tail waved horizontal to the ground as Daddy lifted the kite up over his head.

My heart throbbed as he released the giant structure and it danced toward the clear blue sky. The unexpected force placed on the cord by this behemoth jerked my sixty-pound frame completely off the ground, and the next thing I knew, I was being dragged across the grass. I let go of the spool when I realized what was happening and looked up just in time to see Daddy grabbing for the line as it raced past him.

He got his hands on it just ahead of the spool and held firmly as it spun him around to face the receding craft. He rocked forward slightly as the slack came out of the line, but the sudden stop snapped the horizontal cross brace and the kite folded in the center. Its wounded body fluttered to rest in a tree beside the policeman's shack where it remained throughout the summer as a monument to our grand effort.

Fourteen: **Invasion**

As we stood on the elevated tee overlooking the eighteenth hole waiting for the slow foursome in front of us, a chilling breeze whispered through the pines surrounding our vantage point. The sun had almost set behind us, and the mid-December evening was beginning to exude its cooling, twilight breath. We were finishing our regular Sunday eighteen, racing to beat the impending darkness that would make following a little white ball next to impossible.

Smith was having an exceptionally good day and was well under bogie after seventeen holes. He had the honor on the last hole and was waiting for a clear fairway to launch his last drive of the day. Dr. Cowan was having his typical up and down effort, and I was involved in an uphill struggle to keep my score in double digits for the round.

As we stood there, awaiting Jim's drive, my eyes caught a glimpse of a bat silhouetted against the clear, blue sky. It was darting up and down, circling between the trees that lined our target landing area. This furry mammal was most likely searching for a rare insect that had been awakened from hibernation by the unseasonably warm rays of the afternoon sun on this first official day of winter.

We watched it flittering back and forth, as if bouncing off each puff of air that made its way through the trees on either side of the green expanse before us. It continued to weave away from the tee then back again, well over our heads.

When the fairway cleared, Smith placed his final drive down the middle, well out into the fairway of the five-par hole. John drove his ball to the usual spot into the trees on the right with his patented doctor's slice bouncing across the cart path but stopping short of the out-of-bounds stakes. As I delivered my last effort from the tee, the head of my driver went completely under the ball sending it high into the darkening sky.

As my projectile reached its zenith, the bat somehow found his way back in our direction and began to circle my Top Flight, mistaking it for a bug – a very big bug. It followed the ball, almost to the ground, and then swiftly abandoned the chase returning skyward, undoubtedly in search of more tasty prey.

We watched in wonder as the flying mammal demonstrated its acrobatic maneuvers. Seeing the bat dive, zigzag, and circle, I could not help but think of these little critters that we terrorized back in the Atco Village.

For years we had known that bats inhabited the attic of the house next door to ours where my best friend Boyce Thomas lived. Just after sunset, these furry creatures would exit their living quarters through a hole in the soffits where the front porch joined the rest of the house.

Somebody came up with the bright idea of swatting at them as they made their way into the night sky to scour the village for insects. We first tried tennis rackets, but they were not nearly long enough. As the varmints made their exit from their corner opening, they would dip down a few feet then flitter upward and be off on their mission. Their flight pattern put them several feet above the reach of a tennis or badminton racket. We even tried tossing these implements into the path of the bats, but that only resulted in them getting busted or stuck in a tree.

We tried other approaches and eventually learned that an old cane pole proved both sporting and effective. Its lack of girth made it very difficult to make contact with the dodging target, but its length allowed access into the flight pattern. Night after night we would gather and wait patiently, as the fifty or so bats swooped from the crevice about a minute apart. We took shifts with the pole slapping in fruitless attempts to bring down one of these little, acrobatic vermin.

On occasion, we would get lucky, clip a wing, then have to duck for cover as the critter spiraled around us nearly hitting the ground before regaining its heading and zipping off to join the rest of the hunting party. We did some pretty fancy dancing trying to stay out of harms way after one of these partial hits.

One late July evening we were particularly fortunate and brought down two of these elusive creatures. Then we had to decide what to do with them. A large cardboard box was the only thing available at the time, so we made do with that.

When we carefully opened the confine the next morning, we were disappointed to find that our captives had given up the ghost during the night. We then noticed two tiny forms that looked like miniature, bald monkeys in the bottom of the box. The bats had given birth before they departed this life, and the babies were apparently stillborn. This was a sad moment, but a thirteen-year-old can only grieve so long for a wild beast that had fallen victim to his prowess with the fishing pole.

We buried the two adults and focused our attention on these minute beings. Barely half an inch long, the babies looked remarkably like tiny people. The undeveloped wings resembled arms even down to the fingers on the "hand" the adult has in the bend of each wing. In the early 1950s, there were many reports of UFO's from military and civilian observations. Unidentified flying objects were in the forefront of people's minds, and the media was filled with reported encounters.

In this context, a scheme began to emerge in our evil, early-teen brains, and our ideas fed off each other until we had put the final touches on our plan. It was the beginning of an incident that would be talked about for months to come.

For a couple of years Cliff and I had been hunting snakes at Nancy Creek, a quarter of a mile over the hill behind the village. We had been able to bring home several live specimens to share with our neighbors. A combination of fear and curiosity prevailed in the minds of these observers, and we began to establish quite a reputation for ourselves.

Bill Dyar, Cliff's younger brother by three years, and four of his friends, whom Cliff called the "Little Urchins," decided they wanted to make their mark as intrepid snake catchers, too. They were a bit jealous of the notoriety that we were receiving.

The gallant band would get together toting sticks, nets, gloves, and other snake-catching-looking paraphernalia and head over the hill, through the pine thicket, to the creek. They would always come back with stories of what they had seen that would make most fishing yarns seem like fairy tales.

After ignoring their brazen and obnoxious boasting for a while, we decided maybe we should give them something to brag about. It was time to put our little hoax into action, lest the rest of our days be spent listening to their swaggering.

The scheme we were cooking up involved the two tiny bat babies and a radiosonde we had found the previous summer while snake hunting at Rowland Springs. We spotted this contraption attached to a small, red parachute in a low pine tree on the other side of the creek from Aunt Beck's house, a snaky-looking place where few dared to tread.

I had seen one of these weather-monitoring devices in some long ago Weekly Reader, and knew it should be turned over to the authorities. Upon close examination, however, we discovered that our find far exceeded the return date, so we just added it to our collection of "miscellaneous stuff found in the woods," which included several bleached white turtle shells and an abandoned hornet's nest.

The main section of the radiosonde was a cylinder almost two feet long and a little wider than a soup can with a cone shaped end. A myriad of wires, connectors, tubes, and other cool looking stuff was visible through the heavy, reddish plastic shell. At first glance, it looked a lot like it could certainly be a spacecraft of some description.

Cliff and I decided it was time to remove this trophy from the mantle collection and put it to good use. With a hammer and pliers we knocked a hole in the side exposing the inner workings and ripped out some wires and other parts. We then took a candle and scorched the opening of the cylinder inside and around the gash we had made. We grabbed some props from an old crystal radio kit and headed to the creek, our bat babies carefully wrapped in a handkerchief placed in a matchbox.

We chose a spot at a bend in the shallow waterway where a large, moss covered boulder narrowed the path to only a couple of feet. On a ledge about chest high, we jammed the pointed end of the radiosonde into a shallow crevice. We charred the moss and other plant life clinging to the big rock and sprinkled the other assorted parts around the area.

Then Cliff gently removed and unrolled the handkerchief and placed the two tiny corpses in the soot-laden hole, arranging each as if it were trying to escape from the crashed vehicle. We played around with the position of their bodies and their appendages until the whole scene began to take on an eerie sense of reality.

After setting the stage, we headed back up the hill and settled on Cliff's front porch where we could see the approach to the creek. We sat there for just over an hour when we heard Bill gathering his little band of adventurers. They headed out across the field and through the pines chattering loudly with their snake hunting gear waving in the air.

Then we waited, but not for long.

At first we heard them. Then we caught a glimpse of their empty hands flailing wildly in the air over the hill. As their faces appeared above the horizon, all eyes were wide, each mouth agape and emitting a variety of screams.

They dashed through the field, across Litchfield onto Goodyear Avenue, three houses down from the porch where we were sitting. They ran straight through the village toward the policeman's shack where a patrolman was usually on duty. Their shouts attracted a lot of attention and people began to fall in line behind them, curious as to what was going on.

After a few muffled chuckles, we figured it would probably be prudent to remove any evidence of wrongdoing that could be traced to us, so Cliff and I headed over the hill to the scene of the charade. We gathered the remains of our little caper and retreated up the creek into Wingfoot Park on the other side of Gilliam Springs Road.

We hid the props in a small cave at the far end of the park where we knew they would be safe and headed back toward the village through the pasture on the opposite side of the road, well away from the action. And action there was.

Mr. Padgett, the patrolman on duty at the time, was leading the throng. He had his pistol drawn, waving in the air, and was followed by the kids and a mob of villagers carrying rakes, hoes, axes, and other weapons. It looked like a scene from the old Frankenstein movie sans the flaming torches.

Seeing the disturbance that had ensued, we decided to take a left up Cassville Road instead of returning to the village just yet, circling around behind the elevated railroad bed to stay hidden from view. We followed it to the big trestle over Pettit Creek on the opposite side of the village from Nancy Creek.

Turning right, our path took us down the creek bank through the large pasture and under the bridge on Cassville Road to the small trestle on the spur track that served the mill. We headed back into Atco, as innocent-looking as we could, and immediately saw two of Cartersville's city police cars that had been summoned for this community emergency.

People were still abuzz with their version of the tale, and we heard every imaginable chronicle of the event. It was a true test for us to keep tight-lipped about the whole affair. We knew how much trouble we would be in if we were discovered as the perpetrators of this hoax. I must admit it had gone a lot further than we had ever intended.

Conversation about the incident circulated around the village for a while, but eventually folks came to the conclusion that the kids had made the whole thing up or they had misinterpreted something they saw that day. I can only imagine what went on in our absence that summer afternoon, and to this day, somewhere, there are probably five middle-aged men that know they had a close encounter of "some kind" that day.

Fifteen: **Snake Bit**

We were finishing up our carry-out dinner from Chick-fil-A with my granddaughter Bailey whom we had been feeding on Wednesday nights so her grandmother could go to a yoga class. We cleared the table, and I took down a glass fish bowl that we kept on the mantle over the kitchen fireplace. In it was a new pet that I wanted to show to Bailey.

A week earlier I was walking out of the Country Club on a sticky August night after playing our regular Thursday evening round with several of my golf buddies. In the summer, when daylight savings time is in effect, there is plenty of time to walk nine holes and have dinner together as sort of a boys' night out.

I was the last of our group to leave after making a quick pit stop. As I went out the side door of the club, a slight motion on the walk attracted my attention. It was a small snake hustling across the concrete, heading for the shrubs on the other side.

Almost instinctively, I reached down, grabbed the wiggly form, and picked it up for a closer look. It was a gray rat snake, barely a foot and a half long and about the size of a pinkie finger. It tried a few striking moves to intimidate me, but a specimen this size can't do a lot of damage.

As I held this little creature, I began to think about how I might be able to transport it to our house. Nothing in my minivan, including my golf bag, came to mind as a potential carrying device, so I headed back to the clubhouse.

I asked the first staff person I came to for a "to-go" cup with a lid. I had the little captive out of sight in my right hand at my side in hopes his presence would not cause any trouble. She fetched the requested container, and as I lifted the snake up to place it in the Styrofoam vessel, her eyebrows raised as her gaze fell on my squirmy catch.

She disappeared toward the kitchen and soon returned with several wide-eyed staffers. One by one I let them stroke the scales of this tiny specimen and even a few had the nerve to hold it. All the while, I was giving my spiel about the value of snakes, especially the constrictors like the rat snake, and the contributions they make to society.

When I got home I was not able to find one of the large aquariums we have accumulated over the past several years, so I had to make do with a small, spherical fishbowl that once held a family pet. It was a little cramped, but with the rocks, bark, and pine straw it seemed woodsy enough. There was a sprig from a dead branch of privet hedge that offered many levels to navigate over a small, clay water bowl that was once an ashtray project brought home by one of the kids from art class.

I reached into the tank, gently picked up the rat snake, and placed it on the towel on the table in front of us. It wiggled and squirmed across the table toward Bailey who let out a little squeal and recoiled back into her chair. I grabbed the small varmint and placed it in front of my seat again.

This time it scooted to the left toward Jane, and I intercepted its flight and returned it to the starting position. To the right it went, this time toward the vacant end of the kitchen table. As it made its way off the towel it began to wiggle in place on the polished surface of the slick wood block.

I retrieved it from its futile trek and again placed it on the center of the towel. It took an immediate left toward Jane's folded hands and struck suddenly, without warning, catching the edge of her folded right hand between the little finger and the wrist. And it would not let go.

With eyes as big as the plates we had spread in front of us for our semi-catered dinner, she uttered in a somewhat raised voice, "Is it poisonous?"

I reassured her that it was not and reached over, grabbed the little rascal by its jaws, and pried it from her hand. She was still agape as I transferred the errant captive back into its small abode and looked closely at the wound it had inflicted.

There was a semicircular ring of tiny teeth marks evident on this tender part of her right hand. A tiny bit of blood was seeping out of the two largest prick marks but nothing that looked life threatening, except for the shock of the event.

I still remember the first time I was bitten by one of the captives I held in the cages behind my house in the Atco Mill Village. A neighbor who knew I collected snakes worked for a pulpwood company. As they felled a dead pine tree while clearing the way for a logging road, a king snake was uprooted from its den, and several members of the crew attacked it with axes and other tools they had at their disposal.

This good neighbor rescued the battered reptile and managed to coax it into a burlap sack that happened to be available. The poor animal had several scars on his sleek black and yellow body, and his tail had been severed just south of the business end.

Over the next month or so I was able to nurse this specimen back to a fair degree of health, but the tail would take several years to return to its original state. In the process I was able to tame the critter and could handle him whenever I wanted without fear of attack.

My battered king snake had become so tame that I could, and did on many occasions, wrap his four-foot long body around my neck and walk down the street and into the Atco store. Most folks who saw my pet clinging to my throat assumed it was a toy and would freak out when it flicked out its tongue and moved in such a manner that they could tell it was the real thing.

One afternoon as I was sitting on the concrete bench behind our house, my king pet was crawling between my fingers and up my wrist. All of a sudden he tilted his head sideways and bit on the inside of my elbow.

I instinctively grabbed him and yanked him from my arm with my left hand, and he immediately struck at and connected with the forefinger of that hand. I half dropped, half threw the squirming form into the thick clover bed at my feet and just stared down at his coiled body.

He lay still for a while then slowly turned his head up toward me. As we sat there eye to eye, I could have sworn his eyelids closed half way down in an attempt to apologize for his previous actions and make amends.

I slowly lowered my bare hand down to the ground in front of my old buddy, and after a brief pause, he made his way up between my fingers and coiled around my wrist. He never bit me again or even threatened such. As best I could figure out, I had irritated a tender spot on his still-healing body that caused his retaliation.

I never told my folks about this incident because I knew how they felt about my snake collecting, especially my mother, and this little incident may well have given them cause to insist that I abandon my latest hobby.

I have been bitten a number of times since then but most have been pretty run of the mill bites. A major exception was the wound that was inflicted by a large black snake. He was almost six feet long and "mean as a snake", so to speak.

As with water snakes, this family that includes black racers, blue racers, and coach whips are particularly difficult to tame. The constrictors, like king snakes, rat snakes, and chicken snakes, make much better pets because they can be pretty well trained in a relatively short period. After that they can usually be handled with little fear of being bitten.

Because of his unpleasant disposition, I handled this large racer with my right hand protected by a heavy work glove. One afternoon when I was returning him to his cage he leaped out toward me as I closed the lid. The door caught his body about two-thirds out of the opening, and he began to flail around trying to free himself.

Instinctively, I grabbed for him with both hands, and he scored a perfect hit on my bare left index finger. At the moment of the strike, my limited years of experience completely left me, and I jerked my hand back as quickly as I could. This was a serious mistake. The action left a series of gashes where the razor sharp teeth had ripped through the flesh instead of a neat area of small puncture marks.

An involuntary yelp issued forth from my lips as I made another grab at the reptile, this time with the gloved hand. I was able to wrestle him back into his pen and secure the door as blood streamed down my left arm onto my tee shirt and shorts. I grabbed the injured finger with my other hand and realized I was faced with a little dilemma.

I knew Mama was in the house, but I also knew how she felt about snakes and my collecting such creatures. My choices were very limited: I could stand there and bleed to death, run to the mill to see the first aid nurse, or face the music inside. I chose the latter. I took off my shirt and wrapped it around my hand, which hid a lot of the blood, but a significant amount was evident as I entered the kitchen. As calmly as I could I said, "I hurt my finger."

She looked up from the sink, saw the blood and began to turn a little pale as she asked, "How in the world...?"

"Uh... Uh..." mashed in the door, the bicycle chain, cat scratch, fish hook; a hundred lies flashed through my mind as she stared at the reddening shirt. "Ah, my snake just bit me, that's all," I was finally able to say, as nonchalantly as possible.

"What!" was the immediate reaction followed by a swift grab of the arm and being dragged toward the front of the house. A jumble of words rolled out of her mouth on top of each other that included doctor, ambulance, hospital, poison, emergency, and die. All the while I was in tow.

Half way to the front door I was able to get a word in edgewise and convince her that it was not poisonous, and she began to calm down a little bit. We went back to the kitchen and unrolled the blood-soaked tee shirt from my hand. In all the excitement that followed my announcement, I had forgotten about the pain, but it soon returned as the soap and water washed over the open wound.

In those days, alcohol – the rubbing kind, not the drinking kind – was considered a cure-all for broken skin of any type. And it burned. It burned even when dabbed on with a cotton ball, and here Mama was pouring it into my bleeding finger like milk on corn flakes. I think she had a little punishment in mind almost as much as my well-being.

Following the painful alcohol bath, she wrapped half a roll of sterile gauze around my injury and sealed the deal with what we called adhesive tape. Johnson and Johnson manufactured this product and it came on a thin, white metal spool with a neat clip-off cover that surrounded the perimeter.

Word spread pretty quickly that a snake had bitten me, and the impressive dressing on my left hand added a great deal of credence to the story. It may have been exaggerated a bit as the events were told and retold, but I am sure I had nothing to do with that.

Sixteen: **Teeter Totter**

A new playground was a part of the plan for the Family Life Center that I had the privilege of designing for our church. In one of our meetings, we were discussing this amenity with members of the church staff who administer the Sunday School and Learning Center programs that deal with children. In order to compare the new design with the current play area, I went by the church to measure the present space.

I am always amazed with the new, colorful, plastic equipment that is in use today. It is such a contrast to the old pieces I remember from the Atco Village. Our playground was located on the opposite side of the old school from the swimming pool. Several little league baseball fields have long since replaced all evidence of the school, playground, and ceramic tile-lined pool.

One of our favorite pieces of equipment was the seesaw. This particular model had four boards, each made of full dimension two by tens with little leg cutouts that roughly defined the seats. The boards were attached in the center to a heavy steel pipe that was supported by A-frames of the same material at each end and in the center between the two pairs of boards.

The earth at the ends of the boards was worn down from years and years of use, creating large, rounded depressions in the landing area. These were not very noticeable under normal conditions, but a little shower changed all that. The red clay hollow would hold a muddy puddle presenting an excellent opportunity to make a mess of yourself trying to out splash your partner on the other end.

A handlebar-like assembly consisted of a small piece of pipe coming out of the battleship gray painted board just in front of the seat. This pipe had a tee about a foot off the board surface that held the eight-inch-long pipe handlebars. All parts were well worn from years of use and, except for an occasional splinter, were relatively safe when used as intended.

We, however, did not always use the apparatus as intended. With limited recreational equipment at our disposal, we sometimes became bored with using each in the normal manner. The seesaw was no exception and the creative urge expressed itself as it did with all the other available facilities. One of our optional seesaw activities was a cross between follow-the-leader and chicken. The leader would walk a defined path and the others had to follow, or they would be called the dreaded "chicken." The trek usually started at the grounded end of the first seesaw board. Stepping over the handle, the leader would ease up the slanted plank to the fulcrum and gingerly coax the board to the ground on the opposite side. If he lost his balance or had to use the support pipe to steady himself, he immediately lost his position of leadership.

If he made it through the transition, he would walk down the other side of the board. This was much harder than it looked on the slick, inclined, surface and demanded serious concentration amid the heckling from the other competitors. It was then the next person's turn to match the feat.

The following challenge might begin the same way, but after reaching the center of the board, the leader would find the balance point that held both sides off the ground at a roughly equal distance. He then began spreading his legs carefully using an alternating heel-toe motion while trying to maintain balance and keep the board in a relatively level attitude. After reaching some random target with his feet, he would ease them back to center and re-balance the board. If either side hit the ground during this exercise, he was out.

Next he would take a careful step out onto the smooth, six inch round support pipe in the direction of the adjacent board. After a pause to steady his position, a second bare foot was slowly moved to the slick support and another moment taken to regain his balance.

With arms outstretched, the leader would slide his left foot forward a few inches, then match the movement with the other.

One false move and he could come crashing down straddling the beam and temporarily raising his voice an octave or so. This was a critical and dangerous stage, and everybody held their breath until the leader reached the next board. Even if one could jump clear off the support, the gravel surface would inflict a great deal of pain to your bare feet.

The leader's first step on the next plank had to be just in the right place on the down side of center so he could ease a second foot to the board without it starting to tilt. Once there, he would tip toe forward up the slope until the low side began to rise. He had to be extremely careful or the board would accelerate out of control throwing him to the ground below. This happened quite often and usually resulted in the leader or one of the followers running home wailing for sympathy.

Each time the leader set a new example, contestants had to duplicate the feat. The longer you played, the more interesting it became – and the rules began to change a bit. The taunting that began with the second contestant would grow louder and more boisterous as each participant did his best to complete the challenge. Various obstacles such as sprinkling water on the elements making them more slippery and tossing water-filled balloons at competitors were introduced into the game at times.

Another seesaw activity we enjoyed on a regular basis involved just two people, most of the time. It really had no formal name and we just referred to it as "push and bump." It began using the seesaw in the normal way. The transition into "push and bump" occurred sometimes by accident and sometimes by choice. Instead of cushioning the reaction of the board when it came down on your side by bending your knees, you lift your feet allowing the end to slam against the hard clay. This bump transferred a jar to the one on the other end.

Once the ice was broken, the game would begin. The harder you pushed off from your down position, the more "bump" you got to ride when the other side hit the ground. We had never heard of Isaac Newton's physics, but experience taught us quite a bit about the lever arm. The further you leaned back, the longer lever arm you created, and the faster you would move toward the ground. This acceleration increased the force at which the board struck and the reaction that was transmitted to the opposite side.

My next-door neighbor, Boyce Thomas, and I played this a lot and began to experiment with a few options. When there were three of us, rather than leave someone out, that third person took on the roll of "accelerator." He would stand on the center of the board, straddling the fulcrum, and lean to one side and then the other. If his timing was right, this additional shifted weight enhanced the impact, and you would leave your seat on the board if you didn't fold your legs below it.

Locking you feet under the board required a certain degree of care because if you forgot to release them or were a little too slow, the board would slam down on the bare extremities inflicting great pain and causing almost certain major injury. This didn't have to happen to you but once before you learned the importance of paying close attention to your impending contact with the ground.

Boyce and I were engaged in a rather heated session of this "push and bump" game one warmer-than-usual April afternoon. We had been involved in a little disagreement earlier that day and were taking it out on the seesaw. With each cycle, the intensity steadily increased. The action was becoming so fierce it began to attract the attention of some of the other kids on the playground, and they began to gather around. This resembled what happens when a fistfight broke out somewhere in the village.

The bigger the crowd, the harder we pushed and the higher we bounced, purposely not hanging on with our feet to show off for the growing mob. They began cheering with each new height attained. The louder they got, the more brazen we became, completely losing ourselves in the moment and tossing all caution to the wind.

I saw Boyce's face tighten as he pushed off with all his might in order to settle the issue then and there. He leaned forward just after releasing his mighty thrust, and I leaned back instinctively to distance myself from his reddening face. And guess what? Sir Isaac was right again. Every action *does* have an equal, but opposite, reaction. This time, the velocity of the board had been enhanced by our body positions and the lever principle producing the granddaddy of all bounces.

It happened very fast. Before I knew it, Boyce was flying through the air in my general direction. He had not locked his feet under the board and was in the middle of a giant summersault. He managed to hold on to the handlebars for the first half of his flight, but his sweaty fingers lost their grip at the peak of his rotation.

He landed on his back, just on his side of the board with a loud thud that was followed by an audible gasp from the surrounding onlookers. I looked up the plank at the bottom of his feet and saw him raise his head off of the board and glare, with fury in his eyes, between his dirty, bare soles. I knew it was time to make my exit.

As I slid backwards off my end of the seesaw, all the weight was removed, and, as Newton would have predicted, Boyce's side came crashing down slamming his raised head back against the weathered wood surface. About three bounces later, his cranium contacted the steel handles as gravity inched my opponent's body down the sloping ramp toward Mother Earth.

I knew I was in deep trouble as I took off with the rest of the crowd away from the incident. This was standard procedure in the village when anyone was hurt or in trouble. I vaulted the hedge between the schoolyard and the sidewalk in front of Puritan Street and raced down Clearwater as fast as my bare feet could carry me. I could hear Boyce on my tail as I hit the graveled back alley and closed in on my back door. Once inside, I locked the door as fast as I could, even though we had a longstanding, unwritten agreement that we would never invade the other's place of residence, for any reason.

I didn't venture back out the rest of the day, and by morning all seemed to be forgotten as it was in most instances when one of us had accidentally, or on purpose, wronged the other. We are still good friends after fifty years and manage to get together every several months for a "friendly" round of golf.

Seventeen: **Papa Watkins**

I took my youngest son, Alan, and a buddy of his on a short fishing trip one spring. We rented a cabin at a fishing camp on Lake Weiss just across the state line in Alabama. Lake Weiss is known primarily for its good fishing, unlike our nearby Allatoona Lake, which is not a fisherman's paradise by any stretch of the imagination. Alan has always loved to fish, as have I, even though I have seldom made time to wet a hook in recent years.

We rented an old bass boat and had a lesson on how to start it up for our early morning outing the next day. We managed to oversleep a little but were in the boat about sunrise, anxious to begin our angling adventure. I went through the cranking procedure step by step. It fired up fine, but as soon as I put it in gear, the motor quit. I tried over and over to engage the engine with the same results. We had drifted quite a ways out into the lake in the morning breeze so we had to row back to the dock. I sent Alan to find the attendant to grant us some assistance.

After a long wait, we finally saw Alan coming over the hill with "Bubba", our nautical "engineer." Alan had to wake him up to come assist us, and he said the guy had a wad of Red Man in his cheek when he opened his eyes. In seconds he had us running after adding the one step I had omitted, and we were off and on our way with the sun well up in the hazy sky.

Several hours after we dropped the first hook, we began to realize that fishing was not as easy as we had imagined with three in a boat designed for two. Naturally, the two boys sat in the more comfortable swivel chairs at each end of the boat so they could see and cast in all directions with a simple turn of the body. I was stuck in the middle wooden seat dodging lures and hooks for the better part of the day.

I had forgotten how unstable a boat could feel as you move around to try and find the bait can or reach for the tackle box. The two kids didn't seem to mind the rocking, and they got several good laughs watching my fifty-plus-year-old body trying to navigate around the craft without falling in the lake. It sure was easier and a lot more fun when I was a bit younger.

The situation was only made worse by the fact that the fish simply were not biting, at least not what we were offering. The biggest thing we caught was a turtle with a shell well over a foot across, and he was hooked in the back foot. Even he was not interested in our bait.

During one of many long idle periods between nibbles, we started talking about fishing and where our love of it had come from. I told Alan and his friend about how much my granddaddy had loved the sport. I don't think he ever fished from a boat, but he could sit on the bank of a pond, creek, lake or river from sunup until well after dark without so much as a cork wobble and not get discouraged.

My mother inherited this intense adoration for drowning worms and loved to go whenever she could coerce Daddy into taking her. He enjoyed the activity or at least faked it pretty well to keep Mama happy. At some point he bought a small five-horse-power Johnson outboard motor that was kept in our coalhouse in Atco. Daddy would get me up before daylight, and we would rent a boat at Bill's Boat House and fish all day at Allatoona, but that is another story.

Mama never learned to swim and much preferred to fish from the bank. Daddy finally convinced her that if she wore her life jacket all the time, she would be perfectly safe in a boat. She eventually agreed to try it, but every time the boat would rock a little we could hear her all over the cove fussing at Daddy.

I called my granddaddy Papa. Some of my cousins called him Pap, and still others called him Paps, like the old Blue Ribbon beer. His real name was Frank C. Watkins, Jr. The "C" stood for Claude, and we would kid him off and on about his middle name.

His daddy was obviously the senior and he had served as Justice of the Peace in Bartow County many, many years ago. My cousin Danny, who is a year older than I am, showed up at a

Watkins reunion at Dellinger Park with Grandpa Watkins' original JP seal. He stamped every piece of paper that anybody in the gathered throng could produce, including a few napkins.

Long before Papa died in 1961, during my first quarter at Georgia Tech, he would take me for walks around town and sometimes up to the old courthouse on a hill in the center of the city. His daddy's JP office had been in the basement and there is a set of granite steps that led down to his door. Papa would hang out there waiting for his dad to get off work.

Over time, he and a couple of friends had etched the squares of a checkerboard in the flat, stone cap of the retaining wall. It took them months to do it using flint rocks and taking turns working on one square after the other. They would play checkers there as they waited, and you can still see the faint outline today.

He also showed me the silhouette in the same piece of rock that he had traced around his own hand. When he was there waiting by himself with no checkers partner, he would work on the outline day after day until the likeness was complete. This handprint is still faintly discernable now. Every time we visited the courthouse, he would put his hand over the imprint to prove to me it was his. It did not take long for me to figure out that it matched a lot of hands, but I never doubted that it was genuine.

Papa was a printer by trade. After moving from Cartersville to Acworth in 1945, he helped establish the Acworth Progress, which later became the North Cobb News. He and his son Gene ran the small newspaper for many years. I loved to go there and watch the press roll when it was time to print the weekly rag. After the real paper was completed for the week, he would let me push the big peddle down near the floor with my own foot. This made the huge, round, press head move down as the rollers inked the type and made contact with the newsprint.

I don't remember the details of the press operation, but I will never forget the many drawers of letters in the worktables. The letters were all different sizes, from headlines, down to tiny print, and they all read in reverse. This made it very difficult to distinguish between some, giving rise to the saying, "Mind your p's and q's." Each letter had to be set in place by hand on a large board and clamped in place before the press could run – a task requiring great patience.

Papa smoked Bull Durham tobacco, which he kept in a small bag that fit in his hand. The bag had a thin yellow draw-string that secured the open end. He carried a small, tin box that held his cigarette papers, and he rolled his own. He would hold a tissue flat in his left hand and sprinkle a line of tobacco along its center. He then used his teeth to tighten the draw-string on the pouch and put it back in his vest pocket.

He rolled it with both hands into something that only faintly resembled a cylinder and licked the paper to seam it together. He always managed to get tobacco in his mouth and had to spit it out before lighting up. As he smoked it, large, smoldering pieces of tobacco and paper would float gently down and settle on nearby surfaces. How a major fire was avoided is a great mystery to me.

My uncle Gene, who never married, lived with Papa on Maple Street in Acworth, some twelve miles south of Cartersville on old Highway 41, which is now Route 293. This thoroughfare was our main route to Atlanta and traversed the country from Michigan to Florida with only two lanes, one north and one south. The old two-lane route was replaced by a four-lane version in the late fifties and then by Interstate 75. The trip to Atlanta, which takes forty-five minutes today, was almost a full two-hour drive on the old road.

Papa's house in Acworth sounded like something you might experience in a Tarzan movie. He was so big into fishing that he raised his own bait. Yes, pink worms and red wigglers, night crawlers, spring lizards, a variety of minnows, and crickets all shared Papa's home. He must have had a thousand crickets at any one time on the enclosed back porch. They were kept in boxes with slick, black enamel paint covering the upper half of each side. This was supposed to keep the little critters from crawling out, but a few of the big jumpers escaped with some regularity.

When we drove up in the dirt drive, we could hear the crickets even before the car engine was turned off. It took two rooms with doors closed between you and the chirpers to insulate you enough to have a normal conversation. To be in their space was almost deafening.

We found that a fun thing to do was to clap one time as loud as possible. The crickets would stop their racket for a few seconds then resume it, in unison, as loud as ever. We could clap, slam a door, stomp a foot, or even belch loudly with the same results. We tried to get creative with these noises, but I'd rather not go into some of the methods we tried.

My cousin Danny and I spent many a night at Papa's when we were eight or nine years old. When you were visiting there, the incessant clamor of the crickets made it extremely hard to sleep. Then, when you finally began to get accustomed to the background chatter, one of the runaways that had found its way under our bed would start up with a private serenade in a very loud, irritating voice.

We would turn on the light, crawl under the bed, move the chairs and cedar chest but had little success tracking it down. The little guys were smart, and when we illuminated the room they would stop their singing and pull a disappearing act. It would patiently wait until we got back in bed, turned out the light and were almost asleep again before it would start cranking up again.

In the morning Papa woke us early and, with bleary eyes we would eat the buckwheat pancakes that Gene made. Real butter and thick, maple flavored, Kayro syrup added a touch that was a treat for the palate. I can still remember the smell of those flapjacks today.

After washing down the delicious breakfast with a big glass of milk, Danny and I would help Papa and Gene gather up fishing poles, rods and reels, and every kind of bait you can imagine. We then headed across their street and down the path between two houses that led to Lake Acworth. This reservoir is a part of the Lake Allatoona basin but is separated by a dam below a bridge on the connector from Highway 41 into the small borough. It looked like a normal bridge with no indication that it was on top of a dam. Passing over it always gave me a strange feeling because the water level was higher on one side than on the other.

Once we reached the lake, Danny and I would try fishing with Gene and Papa for a short while but would tire quickly if the fish were not biting. After putting down our poles, we would skip rocks, climb trees, go wading, chase ducks, catch frogs, and whatever else kids do to pass the time at the lake. I always loved to go to Papa's.

Eighteen: **The Hunky Man**

Kroger was packed with New Year's Eve shoppers when Jane and I went in for our normal Saturday trip. We went earlier than usual hoping to avoid the anticipated crowd, but apparently a lot of other people had the same idea. The aisles were clogged with carts, but everyone seemed to still be in the holiday spirit and remained very patient though navigation was tricky.

Usually, when we arrive for our weekly Saturday night date at the grocery store, Jane goes to the right for the produce, and I head left toward the bakery section to meet a little guy in black holding a tray of sample goodies. This day was no different except the mob had already done a job on the platter, and I had to settle for some crumbs from what might have been a coconut pound cake.

After rounding the back of the store for cheese, orange juice, milk and paper towels, I headed for the canned food aisle. There I joined several others in front of the black-eyed peas location staring at the empty shelves where the Bush and Lucks brands normally live. It was obvious that the old superstition about good luck for the upcoming year being attached to this entrée was alive and well. I was able to pick up a large can of southern seasoned turnip greens to substitute for the collard greens that were also missing in action.

I wheeled up to the cash registers to inquire about these missing items to see if there might be some available that had not been placed on the shelf. The answer was what I expected so I turned to continue shopping.

As I did so I caught a glimpse of the young teenagers frantically packing the plastic bags and trying to keep up with the checkout folks. Seeing those kids stuff those bags reminded me of an event that took place a few years earlier.

Back when the standard paper grocery sacks were being replaced with the new thin plastic variety, we were all being urged to recycle; and Jane was really big into that. In addition to our regular kitchen garbage can, we had bins for paper, plastic, glass, aluminum, and cardboard. They occupied a large space along the kitchen wall and always seemed to be in the way. Now the recyclables are sorted at the county center so we have only one bin in addition to the trashcan. We keep newspapers in the den.

Really trying to do her part, Jane started to recycle the bags from the grocery store by placing each of the used ones in a single bag and taking them with her to the store. Apparently it was considerably more difficult to separate the used bags than to fill the new ones that were neatly held open by the dispenser beside the register.

The bag boys would mumble inaudible phrases under their breath when they were unlucky enough to be in Jane's line. Once I was ahead of her reaching the cashier and heard the whispered warning that the "Bag Lady" was coming. The young baggers scurried to reposition themselves in a different checkout line.

On this New Year's Eve I met Jane back in the meat department and shared my plight. She told me not to worry as she held up a large bunch of fresh collard greens she had fought for in produce. After seeing my expression, she promised she would not cook them when I was at home. She also reminded me to pick up a box of fudge bars before we left the store.

As I paced back and forth before the freezer doors I saw a variety of frozen deserts that brought memories of our mobile entrepreneur, the "Hunky Man," who roamed the streets of Atco. During my tenure in the village we had several who served in this capacity, but the one I remember most was a small man just over five feet tall and very slim. Frail is perhaps a more accurate term, and he walked with a limp. Not so much a limp as a slight sideways gait that made it look like he was walking askew from the direction he faced.

He pushed a white cart that stood a little over waist high and a couple of feet wide with a triangular front that came to a rounded point. The main body of the cooler box rested on two large bicycle type wheels at the back and a small tire below the front end that pivoted from side to side. It was out of alignment in the opposite direction from the driver making it look like they were going different ways.

The "Hunky Man" had a cowbell attached to the bar handle that went across the back of the cart. He would ring this low-pitched clanger as he wove his way through the new and old village. We could hear him coming a block away and everyone made a mad dash for his buggy if they could scrape up a nickel. He had Eskimo pies, Popsicles, and my favorite, the Creamsicle, which had an orange Popsicle outer layer frozen around a creamy vanilla center.

Our house had a small entryway with a door to the porch and one to the living room; both stayed open all the time in summer. The screen door opened to the outside and over time became a victim of my sprints to the street when I heard the cowbell beckon. The mesh in the top two thirds of the door bowed out several inches where I would hit it as I ran through the opening and down the steps to the sidewalk.

One hot and muggy July day I heard the bell's tempting summons and made my instinctive dash toward the muffled clang. What I didn't know was that on this particular afternoon, Mama, for some reason, had latched the screen.

I hit my usual spot in the door at full throttle and was greeted by a resistance I had not felt before. My outstretched arms were suddenly being jammed into my shoulders as the fixed screen struggled briefly against the assault, but my momentum was too much for it.

The frame remained in place, but the screen ripped from its lattice support as the upper portion of my body and face slammed through the top section. The cross frame caught me just below the belt line almost converting me to a soprano. I did a complete somersault over the wood slat and landed flat on my back on the wooden porch floor.

I hurt all over. For a minute I could not move any part of my aching body, and I wondered if I might be dead. As I opened my eyes and focused on the torn screen and warped frame, my thought shifted, and I began to wish that I was. I knew this event would mean Daddy making another of his frequent trips out back to fetch a switch from the plum tree. I think we had the only tree in the village that got smaller the longer we lived there.

I survived this incident even with my allowance being slashed from fifty cents a week to a quarter until the cost of the door repair was covered. From then on I exercised a bit more caution when exiting the front door in hot pursuit of the "Hunky Man."

Nineteen: **Special Delivery**

A few of the guys I went to high school with here in our fair city have been playing golf together on Sunday afternoons for several years now. Each of us ended up here with our families and over time we have formed a group of regulars. None of us is very good, but we really enjoy the company and an occasional wager to see who can "out-bad" the others.

A fellow Cartersville High graduate and a good friend during those early years is Ronald Craig. His life's pursuits have taken him to the South Florida area, but his mother still lives here in town. On a recent visit to see her, he was able to play a round of golf with our Sunday hacker group.

During the round, we began to reminisce about the early days, and many memories flooded my brain. Ronald did not live in the Atco Village where I grew up, but his family attended the Methodist Church there. He cut the grass at the church once a week or so for a couple of bucks and would swing by my house so I could help him spend a little of his earnings at the snack bar in the basement of the village store.

One hot July morning, I rode my bicycle over to the church a couple of blocks from home and arrived just as Ronald was finishing up. I adjusted the kickstand, leaned the bike over and walked across the fragrant, fresh-cut lawn to where he was holding the handle of the still whirring mower. He asked me to reach down and pull the wire off the spark plug of the motor to stop it for him.

I bent over reaching for the cable and as I touched the black insulation just above the plug, a powerful shock surged through my body that almost knocked me to the ground. When I regained my senses, the first thing I saw was Ronald doubled over laughing at my reaction and the expression on my face. I chased him around the yard while the mower sat there chattering and swore I would get him back.

I was beginning to become aware of the fruits of his labors and began to think that earning money wasn't such a bad thing. He traveled from town to the Village on an old Bushman motor scooter that looked like a metal box with a rounded rear, a slightly padded seat, a floorboard for your feet, and handle bars. It was ugly. But it was a heck of a lot faster than my bicycle and not nearly as tiring to ride. He did cut quite an image riding up Cassville Road dragging that mower behind him.

Back then we called Cartersville "town" because the Goodyear Mill Village was located two miles outside the city limits. The company owned all the houses and did all the maintenance work including grass cutting and trimming the neat privet hedge that separated the sidewalks from the yards. The village has since been annexed into the city, and the houses have all been sold off to individuals. The whole area has taken on a very different and more diverse look than when all the houses were the same material, style, and white.

Ronald's mobility with that scooter made the heart of a thirteen-year-old flutter with excitement and a deep desire to own a similar device. Back then you didn't have to be sixteen or hold any type of license to drive one of these "pouter-scooters" as we called them.

In order to afford this luxury, I found out that Ronald also had a paper route. As luck would have it he was getting ready to move up to a better neighborhood and his route was coming open. He was looking for a replacement, and I literally jumped at the entrepreneurial opportunity with visions of owning and riding my own motorized two-wheeler.

I was to go with Ronald for the first week and learn the ropes, the route, and the other secrets of being a paperboy in a small town. The first thing I learned was that you had to deliver on your bicycle. His wonderful scooter didn't have the power to pull just Ronald up the hills on his route, much less, Ronald loaded down with newsprint.

I had always assumed that papers came rolled up like when they get delivered to your door. Wrong. As a paperboy, you have to go over to the paper office at about three in the afternoon to roll what seemed like a thousand papers and stretch rubber bands around them. Between breaking the bands and flipping battles with the other eight carriers, the task could take several hours.

Ronald and I finished the Monday edition and stuffed them into the oversized baskets on the front handlebars of our bikes to begin our appointed round. The papers weighed a ton, and it took several spills for me to figure out how to keep the extra weight under control.

Finally we were on our way. We had to peddle our heavy burden about a mile up Tennessee Street to reach the starting point of the route. Even back then drivers seemed to be almost unaware of a poor cyclist, and getting to your work place was quite a challenge.

The first part of the route was relatively flat, and I was beginning to master the art of grabbing a paper out of the basket, tossing it on a porch, and dodging three dogs while pulling my feet up to the seat out of harms way. This was a little difficult when you had to accelerate or stop; but I was getting the hang of it. Then we reached the hills.

Opal Street runs east off Tennessee Street. Actually, it runs more up than east. From the bottom it looks like that first hill you face on a roller coaster minus that little chain that carries you to the top. We had just restocked our baskets for the second half, and I learned real fast you couldn't peddle up this incline. We walked, pushing the bike full of papers from one house to the next kicking away German shepherds and cocker spaniels at every other house along the way.

Finally reaching the summit, we turned north on a pleasantly flat stretch for a very short block, then turned left on Mockingbird Drive. As I looked out ahead of us, it was like topping that first hill of the giant coaster we climbed on Opal Street, and we were about to go straight down to busy Tennessee Street at the bottom.

Panic set in immediately, but Ronald showed me a few life-saving maneuvers with a full basket, to help avoid a headlong lurch down this slope. The zinging and sagging helped a lot, but I was a nervous wreck before we got to the bottom. It felt like my brakes were completely worn out before we reached the safety of the sidewalk below.

Finally, with empty baskets and tired bodies, we rode over to a little store Ronald knew about and bought oatmeal cream pies and chocolate milk in a little bottle that you had to shake violently, because the syrup had all settled to the bottom. That was about the best tasting thing ever, and I still love this combination today.

I was dead tired after riding my bicycle back to the Village and lied to Daddy when he asked how I enjoyed my first day on the job. Judging by the look he gave me, I think he had made a wager with Mama that I would not last very long. He had told me on many occasions what "work" was all about, and based on his "you-know-what"-eaten' grin, I could tell he was thinking, "I told you so." He had been a paperboy growing up.

Things went along about the same until Thursday, which was collection day. Back then, you collected every week, which meant knocking on every door, fighting off every dog, and begging and pleading with customers for their payment or telling them you couldn't bring them any more papers. They all seemed a lot less friendly on Thursday, except for those who pretended not to be at home. It took about twice as long on collection day, but my tutor promised it would get better as I got to know them.

Friday turned out to be a fairly routine round, except for those who had refused to answer the door on Thursday. We made most of the late collections and were able to finish up the day with relatively few surprises. Saturday took on an extra blessing for me that week – no paper.

Then came Sunday. The man of the house expected his Sunday paper to be waiting on the doorstep when he woke up, so he could have something to do while eating his leisurely breakfast as Mama got the kids ready for church. Ronald had forgotten to mention this phase of our mission.

It began at four A.M. with me riding my bike the two miles to town, in pitch black darkness, up Cassville Road with no sidewalks or street lights, but plenty of dogs. I woke them up all along the way, no matter how quietly I tried to pebble my twenty-inch bicycle, and their barking spread the word of my coming to all the houses up ahead.

At the newspaper office, Ronald had already started stuffing the inserts. Yes, even back in those days, Sunday papers had all that advertising that falls out when you try to find the sports section. I had never thought about how it got there and certainly never imagined it was by a bunch of grumpy little seventh graders with half a night's sleep.

The Sunday paper was also four times as big, even without the inserts, as the regular daily. This meant having to return to headquarters many more times for refills and having to go up killer hills with full baskets.

As we headed back to pick up our third load, it began to sprinkle. By the time we got back to the newspaper office, there was a steady rain and I was introduced to another aspect of the paper delivery business: the inclement weather protective canvas. This was placed over the bicycle basket to keep our precious cargo from getting drenched as we transported it to its intended destination.

It also meant riding as close to the customer's porch as possible and hand carrying the news to the driest place you could find, usually behind the screen door. Being new at this form of employment, I had neglected to bring any type of protection for my own body. I returned home in a downpour and resembled a wet rat when I finally arrived. I got there just in time to get ready for Sunday school and church.

I am not sure everyone got his or her paper that Sunday, but I sure got my fill of being a paperboy. I told Ronald that he would have to find another replacement and gave him some lame excuse, like my folks said it was taking too much time away from my "studies".

From that time on, whenever he pulled up on his cute little "scooter-scooter" I just smiled and said to myself I didn't really want one of those stupid little things anyway. My twenty inch bike, with baseball cards supported by clothes pins, flapping in the spokes, was as close to a motorized vehicle as I needed. You know, if I had kept all those cards that my wheels devoured, I could probably have retired in comfort years ago.

Twenty: **Gone Fishing'**

A nearby clap of thunder echoed through the valley three miles north and about a mile below the Blue Ridge Parkway, in the shadow of Mt. Pisgah. The breeze kicked up by the approaching squall was a welcomed relief from the hot and muggy July afternoon. Jane and I were sitting on the porch of our cabin at a small, quaint resort on the outskirts of Asheville, North Carolina. It was the second day of our mini vacation to the mountains that would include our first visit to the Biltmore Estate the following day.

Our vantage point overlooked a shallow basin bordered by a small creek and fully shaded by mature hardwoods. Several picnic tables and a porch swing were positioned on a plateau near the water's edge presenting an inviting venue to sit and read or just listen to the water negotiate the obstacles in its rocky bed.

There were only eight cottages in this family owned and operated resort called Mountain Springs Cabins nestled in the North Carolina Mountains. Each dwelling had a great view of the creek below that ran through the length of the property and an incredible vista in the back including a huge wheat field with a purple mountain backdrop.

Earlier that afternoon while Jane napped; I took my fishing rod and a small carton of red wigglers down to the stream to try my hand at a favorite sport that a busy schedule has pushed aside for many years. There were only a few worms left after a bit of miscommunication with Jane the night before.

I had bought the bait the previous day at our first stop in Elba where we stayed at Lloyd's on the River. The boys and I had stayed there before, and the swift, clear Tuckasegee River running behind the motel was very tempting. This time I came prepared with rod and bait.

The fish were not biting in the fast moving river, or they did not like what I was using for bait, so I had almost a full carton of wigglers when we arrived at the cabin. We were greeted by large, black ants that seemed to be much more attracted to the worms in the canister than the fish had been.

Jane still had her shoes on when we discovered the inducement so I asked her to find a spot outside for the worms that would be in the shade in the morning. Shortly before going to bed, as I rinsed out a cereal bowl, I noticed the empty worm container in the trash.

My wonderful wife thought I had completed my angling efforts and had carefully poured the worms out of the box under a small dogwood just outside the kitchen door, a place that would indeed be in the shade. I got the flashlight out of the van, scurried around in the dark, and was able to retrieve five of the slower escapees that had not yet made it into the pine straw bed.

With these limited resources I made my way downstream to a place where the bed formed a deep pool of almost still water. My expectations were slowly dashed as my cork bobbed time and time again but produced no capture. I sensed the fish might be smaller than I had hoped for, so I put on a tiny hook and baited it with about a quarter of a worm.

This time I had success. When the float began to jiggle, I pulled out what could easily be called a minnow; a sardine would be more like it. I carefully unhooked my tiny quarry and gently released it back into the clear pool. Another quarter of a worm yielded a second similar catch followed by a third and a fourth.

As I started back up the hill to the cabin my mind drifted back to early fishing trips with my dad when Lake Allatoona was only a few years old. We got up early in the morning, sometimes before daylight, and would drive to Bill's Boat House, which was nestled in a cove near the dam across the ridge from Cooper Branch. Toting rods, poles, tackle box, minnow bucket, crickets, worms, and Daddy's five horsepower Johnson motor, we negotiated what seemed like a thousand wooden steps that weaved from the parking lot down to the water level. Dad would rent an old dark green, wooden fishing boat for a dollar a day.

We had a game we played each time we fished that I called "first, most, and biggest." The contest was to see which of us could catch the first fish, the biggest, and who could pull in the greatest number.

I won two out of three on nearly every trip because while Daddy was getting the boat anchored at our first stop, I already had my line in the water with a small hook and a worm and would catch two or three little bream before he could even wet a hook. He finally wised up and changed the rules to only count the fish that were large enough to keep.

Daddy had a big, metal tackle box with an impressive array of lures stacked on several layers that separated as the container was opened. If he told me once he told me about a thousand times to close the latch after using the box. Maybe one out of a hundred times I remembered, and its contents would be dumped in the bottom of the boat on numerous occasions. These were some of the few times I heard him use a bad word, or several, loudly.

Most of the plugs in Daddy's tackle box had an array of treble hooks on the underside and trying to free them from the slats in the boat bottom and from each other would take a significant part of our time on the water. The old wooden boats had a lattice of thin wood planks about an inch apart that rested just above the floor. It was next to impossible to free a three-pronged hook from under or around this assembly.

Late one afternoon after a long meager day of fishing at the lake, we were headed in. As we passed through the broad evening shadow of the upper rim of the giant concrete and steel structure that held the Etowah River at bay, heading for Bill's Boat House to return our craft, a bat flitted above us catching the last rays of the setting sun.

The furry creature continued to hover near us, and all I could think of was finding a great rock to throw and set this guy fluttering; but where does one find a rock in the middle of the lake? Just then my eye caught sight of the Jitterbug lure hanging from the end of my South Bend fiberglass rod, swaying gently with the motion of our craft. I grabbed the reel end and jerked it into the casting position to the sound of Dad asking, "What the heck are you doing?"

"Watch this!" I said, as I flung the plug straight up into the still air right in the path of the small, black form that was circling overhead. The presence of a foreign object in the bat's territory immediately attracted his attention and he began to spiral about the rising bait. The critter followed it through the ascent and continued to circle it as it slowed to begin its journey back down.

I had made the perfect cast – straight up and very high. What I had not considered though, was a very simple rule of physics: "What goes up, must come down." It also follows, that when an object is heaved straight up, it will also come straight down. As the two forms approached the center of our vessel, I realized I had no place to run, being stuck in the three-foot wide seat of a small boat in eighty feet of water.

The hooks rattled loudly as the plug struck the middle seat that was midway between my position and Daddy's. As it bounced from the wooden surface, the bat followed it around in circles between us trying to corner its supper.

By this time, I was swatting my rod at the hovering mammal, and Daddy had picked up the boat paddle, flailing away at the air protecting his area from the attacking beast. All the motion seemed to have the opposite effect from that intended, and the critter continued the assault, going from one end of the boat to the other. Had we not been in the middle of the lake, we would have certainly abandoned ship.

Our furious antics finally convinced the pursuer that we offered nothing to its liking, and it disappeared in the direction of the spotlights around the dam. Daddy got a big kick out of telling this little bat story over and over again, but I didn't think it was so very funny.

I did get the last laugh later that summer on a later outing to Allatoona. We had rented another boat at Bill's Boat House and headed up the channel to Stamp Creek where we occasionally found some decent fishing. I occupied my normal seat in the bow with Daddy seated in the stern operating the five-horse power Johnson outboard motor.

As we eased in to the bank to tie up to a fallen tree, Daddy suddenly said, "Look at that snake!"

My gaze quickly scanned the shoreline but no such animal was in sight.

"In the tree!" he said with a bit more tension in his voice.

As I turned to the right, I found myself eyeball to eyeball with a very large water snake draped around a branch that was approaching my face as the boat drifted below it. This event occurred before I faced, and overcame, my deathly fear of this sleek reptile, and the thought of one made my blood run cold.

About the time I caught sight of the snake, the boat nudged the tree branch, awakening the dozing serpent causing it to drop from the foliage to the safety of the murky water. The only problem was that the boat was between him and his desired place of sanctuary.

In slow motion the writhing form was falling to the floor only inches from my parting knees. Before it hit the slats below me I leaped out of the boat to the opposite side from the tree limb, landing in knee-deep water. As I deserted the craft, the absence of my body in the bow caused it to rise sharply, the stern being strongly influenced by the weight of Daddy and the motor.

Now, when a water snake is threatened and seeking sanctuary, its natural tendency is to scurry downhill. In the present situation, the stern of the boat, the motor, and Daddy were in effect, downhill. And nature took its course.

As the critter passed the middle seat, in one motion Daddy hit the off switch of the engine and exited the drifting craft in much the same manner that I had seconds earlier. The major difference being that he was in chest deep water.

From my vantage point on the muddy bank he looked like a Canadian goose trying to lift off as he flailed his arms in the muddy lake struggling to join me on dry land. He made it to the muddy bank with a hand from me, and together we were able to wrestle the heavy wooden boat to shore after the fleeing reptile disappeared into the water.

By this time we were not much in the mood for fishing, especially Daddy, so we headed back across the channel for a cool, wet ride to return the boat. My dad didn't kid me about the bat episode after that because he knew I had a better fish tale to tell on him.

Twenty-One: **Roller Derby**

He did it. John graduated from Georgia Tech with a degree in electrical engineering in the December ceremony. It took him a little more than regulation, but he stuck with it and we are all very proud of his accomplishment. He was one of the unfortunate few, who were enrolled when the school made the transition from the quarter to the semester system, and this situation cost him several credits.

As he was moving his stuff back into our house after the grand event, I noticed a large, cardboard box with various pieces of sports equipment in it. Out of curiosity, I pulled out several interesting looking items and began to question John as to their identification and how they were used.

It seems he had taken up the sport (or possibly a means of transportation) of inline skating or roller blading. Another one of those California, "What can we think up next?" kind of sports that has made it all the way to the Deep South. This box contained the skates and all the miscellaneous gear that goes along with it.

First out were the "blades" themselves, actually boots with four beautiful plastic wheels attached in a perfectly straight line. Then came the pads, pads of all kinds. There were pads for the knees and elbows, gloves for tender hands, and even a crash helmet with a strap to hold it in place.

My, how times have changed! We had skates back in my days in the Atco Mill Village, but they had little in common with these marvels of modern technology, not to mention the myriad of safety devices to protect the operator from harm.

Our skates were steel, all steel, including the wheels that made a very unique sound as they scooted across the concrete sidewalks and asphalt streets. Every street in the village had a wide sidewalk on each side, and we used them. You walked everywhere you went or rode your bike, or skated.

There were ball bearings in each wheel, which had to be kept well oiled to allow you to move at maximum speed and prevent rust from accumulating which could easily render the skates useless. When the wheels were freshly lubricated, you felt like you were gliding on air, except for the vibration that transferred from the rough pavement directly to your feet and legs through the steel. After an extended period of time zipping around the village, your entire lower body felt almost paralyzed and it took a while to get your feet back under you when you took your skates off.

These skates came in two sizes, baby size and the size that fit everybody else. This could be accomplished by the rather ingenious design of the skate. Each was made up of a rear section that had two wheels mounted to the bottom of the flat, steel pad with a half crescent shaped metal back rim that held your heel. A long strap with holes in it went across the top of your foot and buckled on the other side, holding your heel firmly in contact with the back of skate.

The forward section had two more wheels below the steel frame where the sole of your foot rested, and a pair of adjustable flanges about half an inch wide that could be tightened securely around the sole of the toe of your shoe with a key.

The two halves were held together by a small bolt running through a slot in the front and rear sections, allowing for length adjustments to fit the size of the foot. A wing nut on the underside of the skate was tightened, which held the two parts together – most of the time.

Skating was the only other activity, besides church, that made it necessary to wear shoes in the summer time. Not just any shoes, but leather shoes that had a thick heel and a sole that extended out beyond the side of your foot to be clamped in place by the skate flanges. Shoes were never popular in the village, but skating almost made it worth the pain.

The one item that was essential in those summer months was the skate key. It was worth its weight in gold and, for some strange reason, this simple little device was easily lost. It was similar to the handle of the old-style manual can opener with the end having a rectangular hole formed by four bends in the flat metal. This hole fit over a matching square lug that stuck out from the side of the skate that tightened the clamps around the sole of your shoe holding it in place.

Keeping up with a key was next to impossible. And if you didn't have one or were not skating with someone that did, it was impossible to refit a skate when it became dislodged from your foot. This happened a lot. No matter how firmly you were able to turn the key and secure the clamp, the smallest twig, rock, or uneven sidewalk joint could dislodge your shoe from the skate and you would go sprawling across the concrete.

It was possible to save yourself after loosing a skate, but it took a lot of coordination and a lot more luck. You see, the front of the skate would dislodge easily, but the strap around your ankle would not come off. This meant that even after you mastered slowing down from a high speed while hopping with one foot and rolling with the other, you had to deal with the dislodged skate still attached and flopping around your hopping foot. This was not only painful, but it severely complicated the maneuver intended to bring your body to a halt before crashing to the ground.

We had a big oak tree right in front of our house and the roots had spread under the sidewalk, raising one slab about an inch higher than the other. This was a real hazard as the higher section was on the down hill side so the offset faced up hill. Our house was half a block from the village store and most of the skate traffic from the rest of the hamlet traveled down our hill to that popular destination.

Most of the kids knew about our little speed trap and could negotiate it by slowing down to step over it or jumping at just the right time. Those who miscalculated the lunge – or an occasional visitor – would hit the joint as we sat on the front porch on cool summer evenings. Following an initial clank, the familiar whizzz, whizzz, whizzz of the steel wheels on the concrete, would become more of a whiz-thump, whiz-thump, whiz-thump, accompanied by various expletives as the skater struggled to stay upright; the loosened skate being dragged along by the heel strap and slamming repeatedly against a bare ankle.

When I saw all the pads, helmet, and gloves in John's equipment box, I remembered how we used to skate. In the summer, all the guys wore shorts with no shirt, and the necessary hard leather shoes. Our elbows, knees and the rest of our bodies were totally exposed to the scrapes and bruises presented by the inevitable tumble on the asphalt.

During the summer when skating was at its peak, the powers that existed in the Atco Village did something that was really appreciated by all of us youngsters. Several nights a week, they would set up barricades to cordon off a block long section of street to allow for skating, uninterrupted by automobile traffic. These became gathering areas for great crowds and were popular the whole time I lived there.

The streets were well illuminated for the most part, but there were some rather dark areas between the streetlights. These zones created ideal spots for a rolling game of hide-and-seek and a place where some of the older teens could get in a little smooching.

Tag was a popular game at the makeshift rink and several things would serve as base, depending on who suggested the game. Sometimes it was the barricades that stretched across the street on each side. This made it hard on the person who was "it" because it was so wide and there was one at each end of the field of play. There was always a fire hydrant within the screened area and it was also used as base on occasion. It was a little trickier because you had to cross five feet of sidewalk to get there and negotiate the concrete curb. Nasty things could happen to you if you missed the curb or plowed into the fireplug by accident.

We also played a land version of Black Dog where a person in the middle of the rink shouted some key word and all the other players had to skate past him to the safety of the opposite barricade. As he tagged each one, they became his helpers in catching the others as they tried to scurry between the barricades. More than once, I saw a body slam into the wooden structure as he tried to dodge the hand of his pursuer.

By far, the most popular activity was not actually a game. It was called "crack-the-whip" and involved a skateless individual holding the arm of a person who was the first in a long line of other skaters who followed with hands clasped. We would have anywhere from twenty to thirty people in a line and the longer it got, the more whip there was to crack.

The leader would generally start out pulling the group in a series of slow, undulating turns that widened as the chain accelerated. Then he would head down the street with all in tow and make a wide turn back in the other direction. As the last folks in the line reached the end of the half circle, speeds had increased significantly. Repeating the action faster and faster each time made for a heck of a ride for those at the tail of the whip.

One night, a couple of young kids who were visiting their grandparents in the village asked if they could join the group in this adventure. Being the responsible youth of the village that we were, we invited our guests to be at the end of the line. They gladly accepted and said how happy they were that we were "including them in our fun."

The chain of humanity started slowly, as usual, and gradually sped to its inevitable conclusion. At the first crack of the whip, the newcomers began to scream as they flew around the corner, almost leaving the ground. They were going too fast and afraid to let go and pleaded to halt the play.

Being the generous hosts we were, the leader increased his cadence and on the next turn we were whizzing madly. As the two visitors reached maximum velocity, the concrete curb was suddenly at their feet. The collision sent them flying, literally, head over heels, screaming across the sidewalk and completely over the four-foot high privet hedge that lay beyond it. Their cries could be heard for blocks as we all did what was protocol whenever we heard a loud noise like sirens, screams, adult shouts, police whistle, or when someone got hurt — we left the scene as quickly as possible. In a matter of seconds, the street was clear and quiet except for the moaning coming from the other side of the privet hedge.

I never found out exactly what type injuries were suffered by the visitors, but I don't think they came to see their grandparents again. And I know they did not play crack-the-whip with us a second time.

Twenty-Two: *I Love a Parade*

It was my first session back at yoga class since my hernia surgery three months earlier, and between my old creaky body and an incision that was still sensitive, I was struggling through the regimen. We had just finished our down dogs, up dogs, split dogs, sideways dogs and every other dog but slaw dogs and finally reached the last phase of the session: relaxation. At this point we all find a comfortable spot on our mat with pillows, blankets, and other props and lie still listening to a soft, soothing, female voice guiding us through our time of internal focus.

The tape had just begun when the serenity of the small yoga studio was interrupted by the sound of a distant siren, redirecting my meditation focus momentarily. As I returned to my mind's peaceful state, again the siren broke the stillness. This time it was a little louder and a little closer. I again tried to block the disruptive sound from my tranquil mind.

Then, faintly in the distance, I thought I heard the steady rhythmic beat of drums. Drums? They got louder as the moments passed, and their sound was suddenly again pierced by the shrill echo of the siren.

"Relax, clear your mind," the tape kept repeating along with other soothing syllables, but the growing clamor in the street soon made the gentle voice almost inaudible.

The drums were beating louder and louder as they approached the intersection of Main and Erwin Streets, just three doors down the hill from the yoga center. Then the whistle of a freight train approaching the Main Street crossing on the square, just a block away, joined the cacophony.

It finally all clicked in my not-so-blank-anymore-mind: the siren, the drums, a train – it must be a parade. These rites occur frequently in our small town, and I can't remember one in which a train did not arrive right in the middle. This causes the string of participants in the first half to run off and leave the tail end creating a large gap in the show. Sometimes both ends will stop and do in place, whatever it was they were doing when they were marching, driving, or riding.

The length of this delay can run anywhere from three minutes to twenty, depending on the train's speed and number of cars being dragged along by the engines. There is always the additional possibility that it will stop, which really upsets the apple cart, along with everybody within shouting distance of the cab.

We have a lot of parades in our small town. With four high schools in the county, there seems to be a homecoming parade almost every Friday in October and November. Each class makes a float, usually on a farm trailer or truck bed, that is towed by a tractor or some kind of fancy pick-up truck with streamers of crepe paper draped all over it. The cheerleaders are dressed out in full uniform and are sharing their hurrahs with the crowds lining the sidewalks.

The homecoming court attendants, made up of three young ladies from each class, are riding in either sleek convertibles or in the rumble seats of classic coupes. Each senior player has a sponsor riding in a fancy car with both their names scrawled on pieces of poster board attached to each side. The jersey number of the sponsor's hero is displayed prominently somewhere on the vehicle for all to see.

The Shriners manage to come to town every year or so and put on quite a street show that winds through downtown. With their strange cars, and even stranger dressed clowns, and bare-bellied saber bearers, it is a spectacle you don't want the kids to miss. This group does some very admirable work with children's hospitals all over the country, but when they go on parade, they really know how to let their hair down, what little they have of it.

Another big parade occurs on Independence Day. Lots of decorated trucks, red, white and blue floats, classic cars and horses – many horses. They always go last in the parades and a quick scamper across the street after they have passed will show you exactly the reason why.

This activity also attracts a lot of politicians, especially in an election year. All their supporters gather and walk, drive, or ride through the streets throwing candy to the spectators and touting the qualifications of their candidate. After the procession they all gather at Dellinger Park to kick off the day-long activities with a series of political speeches and hand shaking mixed with music, food, and crafts.

By far the largest of these parades is the annual Christmas event, a tradition for longer than thirty years. It generally takes over an hour to pass our vantage point on Tennessee Street just a block from our house. It includes fire trucks, local school bands, beautiful floats, pickup trucks full of midget team cheerleaders, lines of twirlers, and an array of horses. And of course Santa Claus is the featured attraction.

Many churches create wonderful religious-themed floats stocked with shepherds, angels, wise men, carolers, and hundreds of kids. The message of "Peace on Earth" is presented in a variety of ways and the moving scenes help everyone get into the Christmas spirit.

The industries scattered around the county go all-out for the Christmas Parade. Huge tractor-trailers are decked out with scenes of Christmas present and past. Generators power the vast array of lights and speakers broadcasting the seasonal message. Hundreds of employees and their children huddle together on the floats in the December chill as the parade meanders through our small town.

Riding clubs and stables provide a variety of horses with beautiful saddles and aptly dressed riders to bring up the rear of the spectacle. Some pull historic wagons or carriages with passengers dressed in period costumes. The Clydesdale team and wagon has been a highlight of the celebration since the Anheuser-Busch plant opened here.

The sound effects flooding the yoga studio on this day were being generated by another very popular parade that is dedicated totally to the children. It is called the "Kiddie Day Parade" and was brought to Cartersville by local businessman Art Munn and his wife Opal. They had seen such a parade while visiting relatives in the Northwest and suggested the idea to the Kiwanis Club where Art was a member. That was over fifty years ago, and the Kiddie Day Parade is still one of the highlights of early Fall in our rapidly growing community.

I was too old to participate in the inaugural Kiddie Day Parade, but my brother David, at nine, was just the right age. We lived in the Atco Village at the time and my aunt, who lived with us, Sister, as we all called her, came up with the theme of Hansel and Gretel. Our next-door neighbor, Ann Head, was a year younger than David and was asked if she wanted to be Gretel. She agreed, and Sister set about to make the costumes.

For as long as I can remember, Sister sewed. She had an old Singer machine and spent hours in front of it making a variety of clothes. If I threaded her needle once, I know I threaded it at least a thousand times. I will never forget the patterns printed on tissue paper with letters indicating where things went together that she would unfold and pin to her material for cutting.

For this first parade, she copied the outfits from the pictures in the Golden Book of this Brothers Grimm fairy tale, and they were perfect. David wasn't enamored with the whole idea once he saw the finished product and briefly threatened to boycott. With a lot of coaxing he finally agreed to don the puffy shirt, suspenders, and the wonderful wig Mama managed to rustle up from somewhere.

Daddy took charge of the gingerbread house construction. He located a huge cardboard box and built a frame to support it that fit over our little red Western Flyer wagon. It was the vehicle that I used to collect Coke bottles to take to the store for the deposit – ten cents for a case of twenty-four empties.

We cut out windows on each side and a door at the front. A large painted peppermint stick adorned each side of the front entrance, and real candy, including suckers and candy canes, was taped all over the cardboard gingerbread surface. A cutout of a witch with a pointed hat and a long nose, riding on a broomstick, was mounted to the wagon frame emerging from the front door.

The project was completed just after dark the night before the parade, and the finished product was taken to the front porch of our house in case it rained during the night. We all went to sleep with images of the decorated creation bouncing around in our minds.

We got up early on parade day and began organizing to transport our entry to town for the ten o'clock start. To the dismay of all, our large collie, Butch, had discovered the snacks attached to the cardboard and had sated his sweet tooth. By morning he had managed to eat almost all of the candy treats that had been carefully affixed the night before.

Panic set in immediately. A combination of anger and frustration prevailed momentarily. Then, Daddy, in his cool, fatherly role, headed for the Atco Store only a block away and returned with a sack of replacement candy. In the flurry of activity that ensued, through the combined efforts of our family and Anne's, the float was redecorated and placed on the pick-up truck borrowed from Mr. Floyd.

A careful, but somewhat speedy, drive to town got the two participants and their gingerbread house to the parade staging area just in time for the judging. They took second place in the float category, and David was very happy with the prize money awarded: a silver dollar.

Sister continued to be the star as she crafted outfits for all of our children when they reached the age to participate in this annual event. One year Alan won when he went as "Mr. T" of the "A" Team, back when that was a popular show on television. Sister had matched the outfit perfectly including a stocking over Alan's head to make him bald except for the Mohawk hairdo she fashioned out of black knitting yarn. He donned gold chains that rattled on his bare chest, and his sleeves were stuffed to simulate the muscles sported by his character.

John, our youngest, decided he wanted to be in the parade at the last minute one year. He put on a pair of camouflage pants, jacket, and hat. He wore black boots and carried a plastic rifle strapped to his back. He entered the bicycle category as a soldier of fortune and won third place.

Kathryn and Alan went one year as a couple. The difference being that Kat wore a suit and tie with a pair of boys polished leather shoes and a top hat, and Alan wore a wig, a dress, high heels, and makeup, including bright red lipstick. A pair of large balloons, strategically placed under the dress on his chest, and a smaller pair on his rear to accent his derriere, enhanced his figure.

The last year Michael was eligible to be in the parade as a participant he enlisted the help of a couple of his friends, Lee Perkins and Brad Templeton. Again Sister had come up with the idea for a group entry, this time as the Fruit-of-the-Loom gang. She made a billowing red apple suit for Michael, and Lee and Brad were in jump suits of color matching the purple or green balloons that were attached all over their bodies. Alan, three years younger, marched in front of them wearing a large cardboard cutout of a pair of briefs complete with hand painted seams and stitching front and back. They won second place in the group category that year.

For fifty years now the Kiddie Day Parade has been an event that kids and parents alike look forward to and enjoy. This year's event was no exception, and it seems to grow every year. From tiny kids in strollers to adults that dress up and walk with their children, action figures, and pets, the parade always has something for everyone.

Twenty-Three: **Black Dog**

"Marco…"

"Polo…"

"Marco…"

"Polo…"

The kid's voices rang out as I unloaded my golf clubs from the hatch of my minivan. I had to park in the upper level at the club next to the swimming pool on top of the hill. The shouts emanating from the game players reminded me of the many games the kids and I enjoyed when we went on vacation together and stayed in a place with a pool.

We played Marco Polo and a lot of other games including one where Alan stood on my shoulders, and John stood on Michael's, and we would toss a tennis ball back and forth between the four of us. Trying to stay balanced while throwing and catching the ball was quite a challenge. On occasion we would get a few stares from others at the pool for our acrobatic looking antics.

We tried building towers with John sitting on Kathryn's shoulders, who in turn sat on Alan's, who mounted Michael's. After getting them balanced, I would go under water, squeeze in between Michael's legs, and try to pick them all up on my shoulders. This was never fully successful, but we had a lot of fun and a lot of laughs trying to master it.

Pool games were a big part of our activities at the old Atco swimming pool. I don't think Marco Polo had been invented at the time, but we had our own games that were great distractions to wile away the summer hours. Most were pretty disorganized, but a few actually had rules.

Probably the simplest of our sporting ventures was underwater tag. This was encouraged by the lifeguards due to their strictly enforced, number one rule of no running in the fenced area surrounding the pool. In our game you had to stay in the water at all times, which eliminated foot traffic around the six-foot wide walkway between the pool and the fence.

One would be considered "in the water" even if it was only a foot being dragged along as you slid on your fanny down the tile curb that surrounded the seventy-foot long basin. The only time you could actually leave the water was to dive, using only one foot, over the head of your would-be-tagger as he approached and had you cornered. This caused some discussion, but generally the rule worked well.

More disagreements involved whether or not someone had been tagged. Sprinting along the surface of the water sometimes made it hard to feel the touch being made on you by "it." Including a strong pinch along with the tag would usually rectify this situation. When the person complained about the pinch, he was admitting he had been tagged.

There was a series of numbers inlaid in dark green tile along the length of the pool that were used as boundaries in most of our games. They started five feet from the deep end with the large number five and repeated toward the shallow end in increments of five feet. There was no buoyed rope separating the shallow end as in many pools today, but the number thirty-five occurred at a depth of about five feet, and it was almost always used as the boundary marker for us "big" guys to keep the kiddies out of harm's way.

This magic number formed the out-of-bounds line for our tag games, water polo, and black dog. Underwater tag could be played almost all the time, regardless of how packed the pool was. You just had to be careful not to be under the diving board when some show-off was demonstrating his prowess with a jackknife, swan, or half-gainer.

Water polo was organized by the lifeguard, J. V. Simpson, and usually took place when the pool was open at night. It was well lit from above and had flush mounted lights underwater that provided limited illumination in the deep end where the game was played. Most of the guys were a lot bigger than me, but they let me play because I could swim like a fish and I happened to always be at the pool. I basically lived there all summer long from the time it opened until it closed.

Two goals, a little smaller than basketball backboards, with two-by-four wood supports on the back, fit snuggly over the tile curb securing our target to each side of the pool. There was no net. The object was to hit the board with the soccer-size ball to score a point. This had to be done while treading water since all the action took place inside the magic number thirty-five, meaning you were in at least five foot deep water.

Teams were chosen much like they were for a pickup game of football or basketball and usually numbered seven or eight to a side. The lifeguard stood on the curb under the high dive and served as referee. He kept his whistle, which he used often, in his mouth at all times.

There were not many precise rules to the game, and it was a little like a cross between keep away and water basketball without a hoop. Obviously you couldn't dribble in the water so you just took the ball as close as you could to the goal to take a shot, or you passed it to a teammate when an opposing player started closing in on you.

The one rule that stands out most prominently in my memory was that an adversary could hold you under the water until you released the ball if they could catch you before you had a chance to pass it off. With all the bodies splashing around in the milieu, no one could tell if you had released the ball, and you would be held under until the orb appeared on top of the water. Then you had to struggle to reach the surface between the thrashing bodies to catch a breath before swallowing half the water in the pool.

Water polo and tag provided interesting diversions at the pool, but we spent most of our time playing black dog. This was my favorite game. It could be played with as many people as you wanted, but eight to twelve was ideal. It began with an impromptu sprint across the pool with the last person reaching the other side being "it." This person would yell "black dog" and jump in the water on one side of the pool. The others had to swim past him from the other side and clear the last green line on the pool bottom without being tagged.

The first person touched would be "it" for the next game and joined the black dog team to try and catch the remaining swimmers. As the dog team added more and more bodies to their company, crossing the danger area became increasingly difficult. The most fun was being the very last person trying to negotiate safe passage to the opposite side with all the other players coming to tag you from all directions.

I was younger and smaller than most of the participants, but I could hold my breath longer than most; I didn't smoke like a few of the others did. My favorite ploy was to dive deep and dodge the larger bodies with their arms outstretched by gliding on my back over the tile bottom at the deepest point of the pool. I could out last most of my pursuers, and as they surfaced for a breath, I easily slid under them to the safety of the last green line before breaking the surface.

Late one July afternoon, in the middle of an underwater excursion below the flailing hands of several black dog attackers, the pool was illuminated by a strange glow followed immediately by an even stranger vibration. My first thought was the "A-bomb." In the fifties, at the height of the Cold War, we were constantly being drilled about a possible nuclear attack. The graphic announcements appeared more than any other commercial on our tiny black and white television screen and we were all programmed to duck and cover. The flash and rumble brought images to mind of those frightening warnings.

When I made it to the surface, everybody was running like crazy to the only exit in the fence located below the lifeguard tower. The lifeguard was leading the way, so I assumed that, at that moment that running was not illegal. I quickly joined the stampede headed for the cover of the locker rooms in the basement of the adjacent schoolhouse.

I kept shouting, "What happened? What happened?" Finally, someone glanced over to me and muttered the word "lightening." When in the swimming pool, this word struck almost as much fear into you as did "A-bomb". As it turned out, lightning struck a fence post at the baseball field just the other side of the school building from the pool.

Now this wasn't just any old lightning bolt. It was one of those giant ones that come with no warning from a sky that is only slightly overcast. Apparently it was from a super high cloud that built up an incredibly large charge before it surged several miles to the ground. It was totally unexpected as there were no approaching thunder rumblings or visible clouds that usually precede summer storms.

I was one of the last to exit the water, and the throng of shaking bodies trying to enter the basement was bottlenecked. I decided instead to just make a run for my house that was only a block and a half away. I crossed the street and ran up the back alley to the screened back door in my typical summer garb – bare feet and a bathing suit.

As I came panting into the kitchen, Mama asked me to go out and roll up the windows in our nineteen-fifty-three model Plymouth on the street in front of the house. The car was parked under a huge oak that provided welcome shade during the hot summer months. Air conditioning was still several years away, so we made do with a large window fan that Daddy installed a few years earlier.

As I sped through the living room and out on the porch, Sister yelled at me to come by her room. I stopped, made a U-turn, re-entered the house and stuck my head in her door to see what else might need to be done while I was out.

"I've already rolled the car windows up," she informed me from the bench in front of her old Singer sewing machine.

Relieved of the task, I took no more than three steps back toward the living room when a blinding flash and powerful blast of thunder occurred simultaneously. The entire house shook, and the windows rattled. The concussion in the humid air could literally be felt, and all of us screamed at once.

I jerked around toward the front door, and all I could see was a huge ball of fire out at the street that completely obscured our car parked at the curb. The big oak had taken a direct hit by this second mega-bolt of lightning, and bark was blown off in all directions. The car received only minor damage from the incident, but I am sure I would not have been nearly so lucky had I been outside.

It took a moment to get our wits together as we quickly searched the house to make sure it was not also hit. All seemed to be in order, but the next several minutes were very tense as we huddled in the center hallway which had no windows, waiting for the next lightning strike. It never came and neither did the much-needed rain.

About ten minutes after the hit in front of our house, an ambulance entered the village and sped up Goodyear Avenue in front of our house. Today we mostly ignore a siren, but back then it was big news, and everybody looked out to try and see what was happening.

The siren went silent a block up the street, and my curiosity began to bubble over. Normally, I would be one of the first at the scene, but I was still considerably shaken by recent events. As much as I wanted to see what was going on, I chose to remain inside and find out the details later.

In a few minutes, we heard the siren crank up again and return past our house and out of the village toward the hospital in town. After some inquiries, we found out that the same bolt that hit our oak tree also hit the water line just under its roots, traveled two blocks, and knocked Lloyd Buchanan unconscious while he was washing his car. He was in the hospital for several days, but recovered fully and still lives here in town. I am sure that he will always remember that afternoon. I certainly will.

Twenty-Four: **O Christmas Tree**

There was a chilling December wind stirring the last remaining leaves on the pecan trees as Jane and I half drug and half carried the newly acquired blue spruce around the house to the front door. The cold air made the gloves we were wearing to protect our hands from the needles feel good.

With eleven-foot ceilings in our 1887 antique of a house, anything smaller than a ten-footer looks puny in the corner of the living room. With four kids between us, we always had at least one extra pair of hands available and willing to help with transport and set up of the tree. Just getting it through the front door and making the sharp turn into the living room while lifting it to clear the stair rail and working it around the chandelier above was a real challenge.

The two of us were able to get it through the tight squeezes to its customary spot in the corner between the two pairs of windows. Getting it into the stand and adjusting the thumbscrews to get it plumb went fairly well. Turning it to expose its "best side" took a lot more deliberation than it did physical effort.

My main decorating job is the lights. Several years ago we got almost organized, and when we take the tree down each year, we put each set of lights in a separate plastic grocery bag. After several debates, we now use the tiny multicolored bulbs and we like a lot of them. Being in their own sack helps the untangling task tremendously, but with each string having a hundred lights, some tedium is still involved.

My method involves stretching the strings one at a time from the living room outlet into the den across the hall and plugging them in. I cannot remember a year when all the strings worked, and this time was no exception. An old set we had used for years finally decided to quit, and none of its bulbs would light up.

A trip to the store in the cool evening air temporarily solved the problem. The new set tested out fine so I started the stringing process. It takes a ladder to reach the top third of the large spruce, and I very carefully wind the lights around the tree to achieve even distribution, a priority of mine.

Finished, I called Jane to the living room and plugged in the extension cord. A cheery colorful glow filled the near darkened room. Our first round of "wows" quickly waned as one of the center strands flickered briefly then went out.

After a few mild expletives, we both instinctively began checking the lifeless bulbs to make sure that each was secured in its socket. We adjusted all one hundred lights but to no avail. This set had also given up the ghost, possibly due to a cat with a fetish for gnawing on strings and wires.

"Not to worry," I told Jane as I headed to the back door. "I know right where the Christmas lights are, and I will be back in just a few minutes."

Trying for a record, I dashed into the building supply center and grabbed another set of a hundred "mini" lights. No one was in line at counter twelve so I checked out and was headed home in a flash. I unplugged the tree and together we carefully removed the defective string.

I got the new lights out of the bag and opened the box, ready to complete my appointed task before supper, which was running a bit late already. I headed for the tree with the replacement set and the thought occurred to me to test it before the installation, just in case there was a factory defect or something.

I went back to the outlet near the door and plugged the string in. Suddenly the room was filled with a pleasant blue light. "Blue! What the heck is this?" I stammered. Every light on the new set was blue. In my haste I had grabbed a box that looked like the set I purchased earlier, but all one hundred lights on it were blue. My color blindness obviously contributed to the error.

My choice of words was not so mild this time as I left the house for my third trip to the store. I was tired and hungry and Jane had a nice, hot pot of chili spreading its tempting aroma all over the house.

The tree was eventually illuminated that night and it looked great. We fixed a cup of hot chocolate after supper and collapsed on the sofa in front of the tree. It was truly beautiful. The tiny points of colored light were reflected in the front and side windows making it look three times as large as it really was. The lights plus the blended smell of cocoa mix and a real tree lead me back many years to Christmas memories from the Atco Village.

The weekend after Thanksgiving, in the tradition of a good southern Methodist, we would climb in the car with Daddy and his newly sharpened ax. We went out Mission Road to the Thomas's farm where we would comb the woods and pastures for just the right tree that would become the centerpiece of our celebration. It was usually cold and sometimes raining, but we stuck to the schedule whatever the weather presented for us.

Deciding on the perfect specimen took a bit of deliberation, but, in case of a tie, Daddy had three votes and David and I had only one each. I was given first shot with the hatchet, but after a few licks in the rocky ground, Daddy took over and finished the job before I completely dulled the blade. David was still a little young to chop but helped us drag the tree out of the woods, trying to ride on it mostly.

After felling the near perfect ten-foot cedar, we heaved it on top of the car with the trunk end facing forward and tied strings around it through the front and back doors. The slow drive home was interrupted by occasional stops to check the tree's position and make any necessary adjustments.

Daddy parked in front of the house, and we dragged the new addition up the steps and across the porch. We made a long turn to the left into the living room and through the wide opening to the "front room," as we called it, which was essentially a guest room. There was a large window facing the street where we always positioned the tree and a fireplace in the opposite corner where we hung our stockings.

I went to the back porch with Daddy to make a stand. He used some scrap one-by-fours fastened in an "x" shape with a small piece below each end of the upper board to level it. He sawed the trunk off as flat as he could and used coated box nails to secure the stand to the tree.

The support worked fairly well but did not allow for a water source to keep the tree from drying out. This could be a real hazard as the lights used in those days were about the size of an adult thumb and put off a significant amount of heat. Dried out cedar was prone to catch fire from the hot globes, so care had to be taken to keep the bulbs away from the greenery.

We decorated the tree as a family and always had a great time reminiscing about past holiday events and expressing our requests to Santa Claus. In those days, Santa's helpers sent out a volume from Sears & Roebuck called the "Wish Book." This issue of the regularly delivered catalog had an entire section of toys that would keep one enthralled for hours.

A very special part of our Christmas tradition was the two-hour trip to Atlanta to visit Rich's Toyland. Lincoln logs, electric trains, erector sets, and all types of cycles and sports balls were set out for the enjoyment of us boys, and there was an equally enticing display for the girls. A view from above was provided by a ride on the Pink Pig.

There were beautiful trees all around Toyland, but the one I have always considered the most spectacular was in Atco.

Every year all of the village kids were invited to the annual Christmas gathering in the auditorium on the second floor of the old Atco School building. Early on the Saturday morning before Christmas, we would all pack into the fixed wooden seats staring at a closed curtain with a large white screen in front of it.

After a brief introduction, the same black and white movie we saw every year would flicker to life retelling a visual version of "T'was the Night Before Christmas." The old sixteen-millimeter projector in the aisle would click and clatter making it hard to hear the words that most of us already knew by heart.

The film must have been the northern version because every year Santa was the one who decorated the tree with the snap of his fingers, and, obviously, it was on Christmas Eve, not the week after Thanksgiving. The tree glistened in glorious black and white as Santa did the finger to nose thing and left the chosen house with the familiar, "Merry Christmas to all, and to all a Good Night."

At this point the auditorium was darkened, and following a brief anticipatory pause, the curtain opened revealing the most beautiful tree I have ever seen. It was at least twenty feet tall and hundreds of large, colorful lights were brilliantly reflected in the many layers of icicles that shimmered in the air currents of the parting curtain.

The gathered throng issued a loud and unison "oooh", punctuated by scattered applause, as the incredible tree was revealed. The awe that the tree inspired diverted our attention away from the cozy fireplace on the opposite side of the stage and the bearded figure in the rocking chair. It was Santa Claus. And for us kids it was the real Santa.

Actually, for the time I lived in the village it was Pat Wofford. He played the part perfectly each year with no padding necessary, and his frame captured the essence of jolly old St. Nick. He did, however, have a little help with his hair and beard.

After the program in the auditorium drew to a close, we all lined up and exited down the steps and through a room with tables full of toys on each side. Fire trucks, balls, dolls, and an assortment of great looking stuff presented an opportunity for each to pick his or her favorite from the selection.

After choosing a toy, we were herded out the rear door and given a stocking filled with apples, oranges, and a large variety of nuts tightly enclosed in red webbing. The twine that held the fruit at bay was bound into a loop handle at the top so we could carry it home along with our new toy.

We call them the "good ole days" and I guess, in a way, they were. We didn't have a lot, but what we had meant a great deal to us. A real thank you goes out to the dedicated adults who gave their time purchasing and displaying the gifts and stuffing the stockings. It was a true effort from the heart and made a tremendous difference in the lives of us kids. Those days are indelibly etched forever in the minds of all who shared in this marvelous Christmas moment.

We always spent Christmas together as a family. Gathered around the tree in the front room on Christmas Eve, we would each open one present that arrived in a large box several days earlier from Swansea, South Carolina. It was from Daddy's family that included my grandmother who everyone called Mama Sallie, Aunt Valerie, and Sam Ethridge. Somehow they seemed to know exactly what we wanted, and their gifts ranked at the top of the list, just below Santa's.

On Christmas morning, after spending some time with our newly-acquired toys, we would dress and head out of the village into town to see my cousin Danny Watkins, who is a year older than I am, and his little sister, Janice, a year younger than David. We exchanged gifts and greetings with them then headed down to Marietta to the Bishops and my cousins Sue and Louise. There we were joined by Uncle Gene and Papa, my granddaddy from whom I inherited my blue eyes and color blindness.

We would get back to Atco with just enough time to ride a new bike and ignite some of the fireworks that Santa had lovingly stuffed in my stocking. In the fading light of a chilly December evening, you could hear the sounds of joy from the skaters and bicyclers mixed with pops from cap pistols and cherry bombs that continued until well after the winter sun had set.

ISBN 141209294-9